Races, Types, and Ethnic Groups

the problem
of human variation

STEPHEN MOLNAR
Washington University

GN
62.8
.M64

D1004451

Prentice-Hall, Inc., Englewood Cliffs, New Jersey

Library of Congress Cataloging in Publication Data

MOLNAR, STEPHEN
    Races, types, and ethnic groups

    (Prentice-Hall anthropology series)
    Includes bibliographies and index.
    1. Physical anthropology. 2. Race. I. Title.
GN62.8.M64   573   74–23935
ISBN 0–13–750257–5
ISBN 0–13–750240–0 pbk.

THE PRENTICE-HALL SERIES IN ANTHROPOLOGY
David M. Schneider, Series Editor

© 1975
by Prentice-Hall, Inc., Englewood Cliffs, New Jersey

*All rights reserved. No part of this book may be
reproduced in any form or by any means
without permission in writing from the publisher.*

Printed in the United States of America

10 9 8 7 6 5 4 3 2 1

PRENTICE-HALL INTERNATIONAL, INC., *London*
PRENTICE-HALL OF AUSTRALIA, PTY., LTD., *Sydney*
PRENTICE-HALL OF CANADA, LTD., *Toronto*
PRENTICE-HALL OF INDIA PRIVATE, LIMITED, *New Delhi*
PRENTICE-HALL OF JAPAN, INC., *Tokyo*

Acknowledgment * is made to publishers and individuals for permission to reproduce the following:

Tables 1–3a and 1–3b, copyright © 1950 by Charles C Thomas, Publishers, reprinted by permission of the publisher and Stanley M. Garn. Table 3–6, copyright © 1971 Studies in Anthropology, Case Western Reserve University, reprinted by permission of the publisher. Tables 3–11 and 5–2, from *The Genetics of Human Populations* by L. L. Cavalli-Sforza and W. F. Bodmer, copyright © 1971 by W. H. Freeman and Company. Table 3–12, copyright © 1969 by F. A. Davis, Co., reprinted by permission of the publisher. Tables 3–13 and 3–16, copyright © 1966 by John Wiley & Sons, Inc., reprinted by permission of the publisher. Table 4–2, from "Genetics and the Human Race," W. C. Boyd, *Science,* vol. 140, pp. 1057–1064, Table 2–7 June 1963, copyright 1963 by the American Association for the Advancement of Science and reprinted by permission of the author and publisher. Table 4–3, from B. Glass, et al., "Genetic Drift in a Religious Isolate," AN, LXXXVI, #828 (May–June 1952), Table 1, p. 152, copyright 1952 by the University of Chicago Press and reprinted with their permission. Table 6–1, from Arthur R. Jensen, "How Much Can We Boost IQ and Scholastic Achievement?" Harvard Educational Review, 39, Winter 1969, 1-123, copyright © 1969 by President and Fellows of Harvard College. Table 6–2, copyright © 1967 by McGraw-Hill Book Company, reprinted by permission of the publisher. Table 7–1, from *Human Ecology: Problems and Solutions* by Paul R. Ehrlich, Anne A. Ehrlich and John P. Holdren, copyright © 1973 by W. H. Freeman and Company. Table 7–2, copyright © 1968 by the United Nations, reprinted by permission of the publisher. Table 7–8, copyright © 1961 by the World Health Organization, reprinted by permission of the publisher.

Figure 1–8, copyright © 1969 by Charles C Thomas, Publisher, reprinted by permission of the publisher. Figure 1–9, from *Man's Evolution* (New York: The Macmillan Publishing Co., Inc., 1965), © 1965 by C. Loring Brace and M. F. Ashley Montagu, reprinted by permission of the publisher. Figures 2–4 and 2–6, Victor A. McKusick, *Human Genetics,* copyright © 1969 by Prentice-Hall, Inc., reprinted by permission of the publisher. Figure 3–5, from *Rh: Its Relation to Congenital Hemolytic Diseases and to Intragroup Transfusion Reactions* by E. L. Potter, copyright © 1947 by Year Book Medical Publishers, Inc., Chicago, used by permission. Figures 3–6 and 4–4, copyright © 1966 by John Wiley & Sons, Inc., reprinted by permission of the publisher. Figure 3–7, from *Heredity, Evolution, and Society* by I. Michael Lerner, copyright © 1968 by W. H. Freeman and Company. Figure 4–5, reprinted by permission of Marshall Newman. Figure 5–1, from *Applications of Germicidal, Erythemal, and Infrared Energy* by M. Luckeish, © 1946 and reprinted by permission of D. Van Nostrand Company. Figure 5–2, copyright © 1962 by Stony Brook Foundation, Inc., reprinted by permission of *The Quarterly Review of Biology.* Figure 5–4, copyright © 1963 by the Royal Anthropological Institute of Great Britain and Ireland, reprinted by permission of

* Full bibliographical data for each work from which use of a figure, table, or quotation has been made can be found in the reference section at the end of the chapter in which the material appears.

the publisher. Figure 5–5, copyright © 1966 by the World Health Organization, reprinted by permission of the publisher. Figure 5–6, from Frank B. Livingstone, *Abnormal Hemoglobins in Human Populations* (Chicago: Aldine Publishing Company, 1967), copyright © 1967 by Frank B. Livingstone, and reprinted by permission of the author and Aldine Publishing Company. Figure 5–7, copyright © 1954 by the Wistar Institute Press, reprinted by permission of the publisher. Figure 5–9, copyright © 1971 by Random House, Inc., reprinted by permission of the publisher. Figure 5–10, from *The Genetics of Human Population* by L. L. Cavalli-Sforza and W. F. Bodmer, copyright © 1971 by W. H. Freeman and Company. Figures 6–1 and 6–3, from Walter F. Bodmer and Luigi Luca Cavalli-Sforza, "Intelligence and Race," © 1970 by Scientific American Inc., all rights reserved. Figure 6–2, copyright © 1951 by Annals of Eugenics, reprinted by permission of the publisher. Figure 6–4, copyright © 1967 by McGraw-Hill Book Company, reprinted by permission of the publisher. Figures 7–2 and 7–3, from Tomas Frejka, "The Prospects for a Stationary World Population," © 1973 by Scientific American Inc., all rights reserved.

The quotations from Hiernaux, Livingstone, Barnicot, and Washburn that appear in Ashley Montagu, Ed., *The Concept of Race,* copyright © 1964 by Ashley Montagu and reprinted with his permission. The material from C. S. Coon, S. M. Garn, and J. B. Birdsell, *Races: A Study of the Problems of Race Formation in Man,* copyright © 1950 by Charles C Thomas, Publisher and reprinted with the permission of the publisher. The quotations from Dobzhansky, Scott, and Gordon from Edmund W. Gordon, "Discussion" in Margaret Mead, Theodosius Dobzhansky, Ethel Tobach, and Robert E. Light, Eds., *Science and the Concept of Race,* copyright © 1969 by Columbia University Press and reprinted with the permission of the publisher. The quotations from Hiernaux, Dobzhansky, Osborn, and Pettigrew from *The Biological and Social Meaning of Race,* edited by Richard H. Osborne (San Francisco: W. H. Freeman and Company, 1971). The review of *Compilation of Common Physical Measurements on Adult Males of Various Races,* by Wilton M. Krogman, reproduced by permission of the American Anthropological Association from *The American Anthropologist,* vol. 73, no. 2. Excerpts from Richard Lewontin, "The Nature of Human Variation," reprinted from *Engineering and Science* magazine, April 1970, published at The California Institute of Technology. Excerpts from *Race and Reality,* copyright © 1967 by Carleton Putnam and reprinted with his permission. Excerpts from William Shockley, "Dysgenics, Geneticity, Raceology: A Challenge to the Intellectual Responsibility of Educators," *Phi Delta Kappan,* 53(5): 297–307, copyright © 1972 by Phi Delta Kappa, Inc., and reprinted with permission of the publisher. The quotations from Blumenbach and Buffon in J. S. Slotkin, Ed., *Readings in Early Anthropology,* copyright © 1965 by Wenner-Gren Foundation for Anthropological Research, Inc., and reprinted with the permission of the Aldine Publishing Company. Excerpts from Arthur R. Jensen, "How Much Can We Boost IQ and Scholastic Achievement?" *Harvard Educational Review* 39, Winter 1969, 1–123, copyright © 1969 by President and Fellows of Harvard College.

TO IVA,
who worked so hard to make this book possible.

Contents

Tables

Figures

Preface

The frequently revived argument over the existence or non-existence of human races serves to emphasize the concern with and recognition of the biological diversity of our species. However, too often such arguments over taxonomic questions obscure many of the details of human variation. Attempts to draw boundaries around groups (racial or ethnic) frequently become ends in themselves. The range of biological and environmental variability together with questions of natural selection frequently are overlooked or are diminished in their importance. In this book I make an attempt to take a balanced approach to the study of human variation and recognition is given to those factors that influence the composition of our species.

This is a book about human biological diversity. It discusses many of the characteristics that show a wide variation throughout *H. sapiens*. The effects of natural selection on these traits are considered and the influences of population size, migration, and history are recognized. Chapter two provides the basic background of biological principles and chapter three describes many of the better known characteristics of anatomy and physiology that vary widely between populations. Several explanations for the variation are considered in chapter five. Questions of taxonomy are not ignored but are placed in proper perspective in chapters one and four. These questions are considered because they are useful in understanding the adaptive significance of human variation.

Many books have been written that trace the history of the "race concept," offering detailed outlines of racial prejudice. Though highly interesting, often as insights into the influence of the intellectual climate upon biological studies, historical treatments of racial schemes have limited bearing on human adaptation. Since I am attempting to describe man in relationship to his environment in a biological sense only a brief outline of racial thought is offered. This outline provides the basis for what I believe to be the faulty perception of human differences that results in a lack of appreciation for biological diversity.

Faulty perception and the lack of understanding of human differences is nowhere better illustrated than in the case of the current arguments over the possible mental inferiority of certain groups. Volumes of material have been written supporting the pro and con of the "race-I.Q. question." These writings take different positions, supporting or attacking in different degrees the proposition that mental ability (as measured by I.Q. tests) is inherited and that certain groups, because of genetic composition, are innately inferior. This book in no way pretends to deal exhaustively with this question. Rather, I describe what may be considered the main points of the "Race and Mental Ability" question in chapter six. These are dealt with from the perspective of the entire range of human diversity and also considers our perception of this range.

Given certain conditions, where does our species go from here? Do we remain essentially the same in composition. Will the same distribution of characteristics be maintained? These questions are considered in chapter seven. Also in this final chapter a brief review of some of the factors important in past populations is made to establish a perspective for future predictions.

Finally, this book makes no pretense at being a complete treatment of human biology. It would have had to be many times as large to do this. However, I do attempt to give a balanced treatment to the frequently discussed questions of human diversity. Bibliographic references are offered at the end of each chapter suggesting additional reading for in-depth studies of the several areas. The book is designed for the student who is interested in the subject but who lacks biological training. It is hoped that this book will also prove useful to those in the life sciences who wish an overview of our species variability in relation to time and environment.

STEPHEN MOLNAR

chapter one

The Ways Men Vary—
Perception
of
Human Differences

DOES MAN VARY?—AN INTRODUCTION

No argument has ever been advanced by any reasonable man against the fact of differences among men. The whole argument is about what differences exist and how they are to be gauged. (Jacques Barzun, 1965: 201)

There is no doubt about the fact of human variability. The usual division of our species into races, however, often depends upon a faulty perception of human differences: we rely on a simple visual appraisal to determine the distinctions between various groups. But even this simple appraisal suggests that *Homo sapiens* consists of a large number of diverse populations whose range of variability is enormous (Figures 1-1 through 1-6). Such variety causes one to ponder the composition of our species and its origin and casts doubt on any scheme which attempts to divide mankind into a few definite races or ethnic groups.

Some of the biggest differences exist in the color of the skin, since people range in pigmentation from a very pale color, as in Northern Europeans, to the extremely dark brown of peoples of the African Congo or New Guinea. Human stature also ranges widely—from the four and a half foot pygmies in Africa and Oceania to the six and a half foot Nilotic

1

FIGURES 1-1 TO 1-6

1-1 An Australian Aborigine. *Courtesy of the American Museum of Natural History.* 1-2 Ainu from Hokkaido. *Courtesy of John Bennett.* 1-3 A Samoan. *Courtesy of the American Museum of Natural History.*

1-4 Singhalese of Ceylon. *Courtesy of the American Museum of Natural History.* 1-5 Bushman of the Kalahari, South Africa. *Courtesy of the American Museum of Natural History.* 1-6 Eskimo of Siberia. *Courtesy of the American Museum of Natural History.*

peoples of East Africa. Europeans themselves vary from short in southern Europe to tall in northwestern Europe. Hair form, another trait that attracts a great deal of attention, varies from straight and long to short and spiral shaped.

Other differences are not so readily identifiable but with some care can be measured. For example, the size and form of the human face differs considerably throughout the world, and the proportions of the lower limbs and the trunk vary over a broad range. Many more subtle differences between human populations, such as types and quantities of blood enzymes, blood groups, and other biochemical factors, can be determined only with the aid of laboratory instruments, but they exist nonetheless.

Just why is man such an extremely polymorphic, polytypic species? Why are these characteristic distinctions distributed among the world's peoples in the way they are?

Human variability appears to be the result of a number of forces that have been at work throughout man's evolutionary history. The influences that formed our species are part of the same complex of factors that gave rise to modern diversity. Each population reflects a number of elements in the environment which have been shaping the population through time. Evolution is still proceeding and may give rise to future populations different from those of today. The composition of racial groups, as we define them now, will undoubtedly change considerably.

How does man become aware of this variation among his own kind? How do we become conscious of the distinct varieties of *Homo sapiens* and their place among living organisms in the world? This awareness developed gradually as a result of extensive explorations of the world by Europeans during recent centuries. Explorers brought back specimens of plants and animals unknown in Europe, and these, together with the stories of strange peoples, awakened Europeans to diversity in the living world—and placed a tremendous burden on accepted beliefs. The idea that man descended from an original pair was especially hard to accept after the discovery of such different kinds of man as the Hottentots, Pygmies, and Melanesians. Natural scientists worked out compromises, often by placing these strange peoples in subhuman categories and depicting them as only partially formed *Homo sapiens*—formulating the concept of life as a web or chain with many links. This "great chain of being" arrangement involved a scale of organization running from inanimate to animate bodies; the animates ran from lower forms through degrees of increasing complexity and finally to man.

This "chain" concept fostered a belief that no two varieties of man could occupy the same developmental level. So, when the Hottentots and Bushmen were discovered, their appearance and language, which the European explorers considered to be like the chatter of monkeys, caused them to be placed in a lower category, nearly subhuman. Later, in the last half of the nineteenth century, when Darwin's evolutionary theory was gaining acceptance, the varieties of man were thought to represent past stages of development. But, even before Darwin, there was a firmly held belief that many ancestral human pairs were created, each differing externally and internally in a way which suited them for a particular environment. These arrangements of man into varieties were frequently complicated by the scientists' personal biases. They often felt that certain groups had been retarded in their progress towards civilization by environmental conditions. Naturally, since these schemes were proposed by Europeans, the Caucasians were considered to be thousands of years ahead of the other races and far superior.[1] Later, as studies of human diversity intensified in the nineteenth century, even European populations were divided into ethnic groups or races, the classic divisions being *Nordic, Alpine,* and *Mediterranean.*[2]

During the nineteenth century several attempts were made to introduce scientific method into the study of human diversity in the form of mathematical analysis. Quetelet, an astronomer, applied statistical methods to the study of human groups; he is, perhaps, responsible for the concept of the average man. But the notion that there existed an ideal, normal, or average is very old. The need to bring order out of the chaos of the natural world has, for many hundreds of years, motivated man to seek patterns and to establish categories. These categories were organized and identified in terms of an ideal type of individual, supposedly representative of the group.

These "ideal types" work well for sorting out widely differing groups such as birds or butterflies or fish, though dealing with units or groups of similar organisms becomes more difficult. This difficulty increases when we search for forms that match notions of the ideal specimen, a factor which has caused many problems in studies of human evolution. Often the investigator had in mind an image of what the type specimen should look like and then searched until it was found. Kretschmer, for example, emphasized in 1930 that his typological system was based on the most beautiful specimens, the rare and happy finds.

---

[1] This idea persists today, as the following quotations illustrate:

"As far as we know now, the Congoid line started on the same evolutionary level as the Eurasiatic ones in the Early Middle Pleistocene and then stood still for a half million years, after which Negroes and Pygmies appeared as if out of nowhere." (Carleton Coon, 1962: 659)

"Great Scott! How many times must I point out that you do not need to use either that word or that concept! The Negro is a younger race. The public has been deceived as to this fact." (Carleton Putnam, 1967: 165)

[2] See W. Z. Ripley, *The Races of Europe, A Sociological Study* (New York: Appleton, 1899).

Subjectivity of this kind has plagued natural science since the earliest times and still persists. The ensuing, confusing multitude of typological systems has made it especially difficult to study our species and our position in the natural world.

Often physical traits are confused with cultural habits of dress or language, which can be useful devices for identifying human populations but should never be applied as if they had biological meaning.[3] A classic example was the term Aryan, which originally was applied to a group of languages by Mueller in 1880. But many writers insisted on using this term as if it described a biological unit, even though Aryan, as used by Mueller, included groups as diverse as the Veddas in southern India, western Asians, and Europeans.

Human groupings, or races, are often socially or culturally determined. Even though these groupings are just as real to the observer as any biological fact, explanations of biological variability should not be offered on this basis. Regardless, racial divisions often are described by such popularized terms as European, Negro, or Jewish; each includes many populations of numerous diverse characteristics. This mixing of units—the confusion between biological and social traits—poses one of the biggest problems for the anthropologist today. It is partially founded in the assumption that certain basic units of mankind are of great antiquity. The result can be seen in the many schemes that have been offered for sorting out our species (see Table 1-1).

The problem is not whether man varies; of course he does; in fact, our species is very polymorphic and few arguments have ever been advanced against this fact. But this variation is not always in the ways that have been described or supposed, because of the impressionistic means by which we usually perceive human differences. The problem lies in the degree of differences that exist and how they are to be evaluated. Human variation seems almost limitless and at times random, but there are limits, often within well-defined boundaries. What are these boundaries—and how do they relate to man's past and to human survival?

HOW DO MEN VARY?

The classification of man as part of the primate order developed out of the original taxonomy of Linneaus in 1735 (see Table 1-2). The placing of man and the apes into the same superfamily caused endless

[3] C. D. Darlington claimed there was a parallel between the frequency of type O blood in a population and their ability to pronounce the *Th* sound. This speculation has not held up on more thorough investigation. See "The genetic component of language," *Heredity,* 1: 269–286, 1947.

TABLE 1-1

Early Racial Classifications

Linneaus (1735)	Buffon (1749)
American (Reddish)	Laplander
European (White)	Tartar
Asiatic (Yellow)	South Asiatic
Negro (Black)	European
	Ethiopian
Blumenbach[a] (1781)	American
Caucasoid	**Cuvier (1790)**
Mongoloid	
American Indian	Caucasoid
Ethiopian	Mongoloid
Malay	Negroid

[a]This scheme for racial division was an expansion of his earlier one (1770). As he described the problem: "Formerly in the first edition of this work I divided all mankind into four varieties but after I had more accurately investigated the different nations of Eastern Asia and America; and, so to speak, looked at them more closely, I was compelled to give up that division, and to place in its stead the following five varieties as more consonant to nature." [J. F. Blumenbach, *Readings in Early Anthropology,* ed. J. S. Slotkin (New York: Viking Fund Publications, 1965), pp. 187-191]

discussions at first, since such a taxonomic scheme implied a common ancestor sometime before the two groups branched off. Figure 1-7 gives an overview of man's evolution based on the wealth of recently discovered fossil hominid materials. This figure illustrates that the results of human evolution are not a few specific types or races of modern *Homo sapiens* but the broad spectrum of variability seen among living peoples today. This diversity makes any simple grouping of mankind into a few categories extremely difficult, a fact we can appreciate today, but natural scientists of the eighteenth and nineteenth centuries were handicapped by the limited data at their command.

One of the basic questions facing the nineteenth-century scientist was whether these strange groups, recently contacted by explorers and travelers, were the same or separate species. The numerous approaches to the problem could be generally divided into two schools of thought. The monogenists believed that all men were derived from the same ancestral stock or the original pair, while the polygenists held that each race was created separately. The argument raged throughout most of the eighteenth and nineteenth centuries, with religious doctrine dictating the belief in human equality—a belief which had to be balanced against political and economic demands of the times. Gradually, the varieties of man began to be understood as a result of degeneration from a primordial type.

TABLE 1-2

Classification of Primates

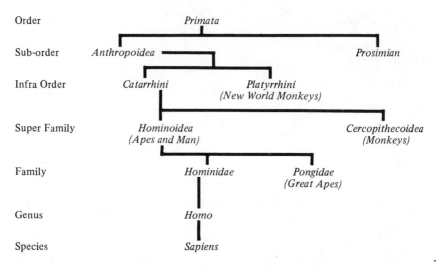

Many classifications were developed in order to subdivide mankind. Most of these followed Linneaus' taxonomic scheme, but many were founded on the assumption that the white or Caucasoid was the furthest advanced. The implication was that only this group was capable of developing higher civilizations. Sometimes such a belief was stated flatly, as it was by Morton, who described the chief physical and "moral" characteristic of each race.[4] He noted that the Caucasian was distinguished for the highest intellectual endowments, while the Mongoloid was ingenious, imitative, and highly susceptible to cultivation.

These earliest classifications were determined by easily perceived biological differences. The criteria were mainly a comparison of skin color, but often the shape of the face and skull were used. The form and size of the skull was an especially popular method for racial studies, because ancient populations could be studied and supposed racial affinities could be determined from their skeletal remains. Often stature, hair form, and shape of the nose were used. Frequently, these traits were applied in combination in an effort to precisely distinguish between populations. However, a large subjective component in each of these classifications led certain earlier workers to suggest that racial classification was unimportant. Also, the fact that all races could freely interbreed made it clear that no group could be very far removed from the original form of the species.

4 Samuel G. Morton, *Crania Americana* (Philadelphia, 1839).

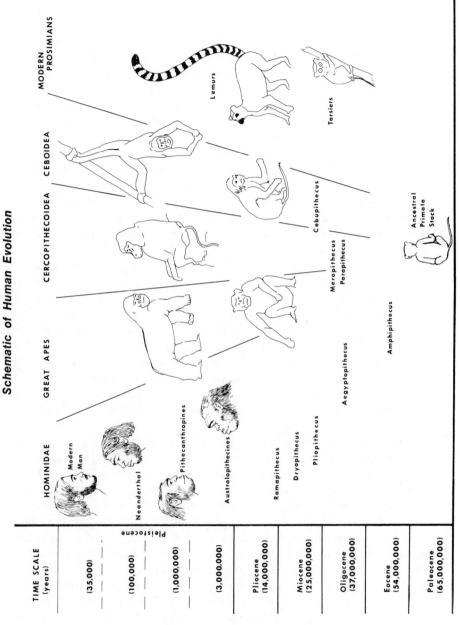

FIGURE 1-7

Schematic of Human Evolution

These factors, plus the variety of classification schemes, made the polygenist view very difficult to support.[5]

Along with skin color, the obvious means of dividing the human species, stature has been frequently applied to establish race groupings. Stature was supposed, at one time, to be inherited and uninfluenced by environment. In the mid-nineteenth century, for example, the French military lowered their height requirements for army recruits because of a general trend in the population; this decline in stature of French males was explained as a result of race degeneration. Since stature was considered a racial characteristic, the effects of undernourishment and an environment changing with the industrial revolution were not considered.

Anthropometry reached its maximum application during the last quarter of the nineteenth century with the development of the field which studied the body form of the living (somatology). With the expansion of a standard identification technique, somatology was directed towards the study of the physique of convicted criminals, the assumption being that crimes were committed by biologically inferior persons. This school of thought was based mostly on the works of an Italian physician, Lombroso, who expounded the theory of the "born criminal." Through his extensive publications he cited a large list of "abnormalities"—such conditions as receding forehead, large ears, square and projecting chin, broad cheek bones, left-handedness, deficient olfactory and taste organs, and exhibitionism evidenced by addiction to tattooings. A person displaying five or more of these conditions, according to Lombroso, was a criminal type. For a time criminal anthropometry as well as the more generally applied somatology were widely used, and vast numbers of people were studied in order to interpret behavior from an analysis of physique. Though this idea tends to linger on, no evidence now supports Lombroso's basic assumptions.

The skeletal system offered many features that could be used to differentiate between populations, and it had the advantage of allowing comparative studies of extinct peoples. Many investigators gathered large skeletal collections from all over the world and, through exhaustive study, managed to sort out what they felt were the most significant divisions of mankind. Blumenbach, a German physician (1752–1840) quoted earlier, believed that the shape of the skull was a significant racial trait; it has often been regarded as highly resistant to environmental influences (see Chapter 3). In the United States Morton accumulated a large collection of skulls, a majority from the different tribes of American Indians. He published an extensive report on his studies in *Crania Americana* (1839). By careful measurement of the internal capacity of each skull, he sorted

[5] For an excellent treatment of the problem see William R. Stanton, *The Leopard's Spots: Scientific Attitudes toward Race in America, 1815–59* (Chicago: University of Chicago Press, 1960).

his collection into five races, comparable to the divisions made by Blumenbach (see Table 1-1). Since in his collections the Caucasoids had the largest cranial capacity, he concluded that they were the most intelligent race—a contention brought up repeatedly in the century that followed.

Blumenbach compared the shape of the top of the skull as viewed by placing the skull on the floor between the feet of the investigator, and Morton relied a great deal on the measurement of skull volume. In 1842 Anders Retzius began determining the ratio between the length and the breadth of the cranial vault of the skull. He referred to this ratio as the *cephalic index* and divided his collection of European skulls into dolichocephalic (or long-headed), mesocephalic (medium-headed), and brachycephalic (broad-headed) groups. Retzius also described two types of face forms, orthognathic and prognathic. Face form together with the cephalic index provided him with a means to divide European populations into four possible groups. Comparing cephalic indices between populations, he found a difference between the skulls of Finnish and Swedish populations. The Finns were considered an indigenous race, while the Swedes had supposedly descended from Indo-Europeans who invaded Europe from western Asia. Overall, the cephalic index has had a long period of popularity and has been widely applied in studies of human variation up to the mid-twentieth century. However, regardless of method used, the human skull's shape has often been regarded as a feature of man's anatomy that was most resistant to environmental influences (see Chapter 3).

No review of craniology would be complete without a mention of Paul Broca (1824–1880). He believed that the measured shape of the skull was the best indicator of the quality of the brain. The concern with brain contents, and hence craniology as Broca developed it, was based on an interest in racial differences, which he believed to be primordial. He assumed that since racial differences find their expression in behavior, the brain has something to do with race (an assumption very much with us today, as we will see later). Broca worked with great care and treated his measurements with a fine precision. He did not stop with a mere numerical descriptive system but deduced from his measurements the racial history or even the social status of the group under study. He translated skull dimensions into a series of mathematical indices and then deduced the personality and even social attitudes of the long dead individual, together with his supposed biological affinities. However, after years of such endeavors he admitted that no single criterion could separate the races of mankind.

The greatest errors in classificatory schemes are (1) to expect all characteristics to be shared by all members of the same group and (2) to mix unrelated characteristics as in the case of Lombroso and his criminal types. Such "types" are no more real than the "average man." However, the simple visual appraisals often involve this sort of error. These distinctions, based on limited information, lead us to make faulty groupings of mankind and faulty assumptions about the "worth" of these groups. The criteria we may use are not related as we imagine. Nose form and head shape or stature, for example, are little correlated; and the skin color of the world's peoples has its own special relationship to the environment.

An outstanding development of the twentieth century has been the replacement of typological thinking with a populationist approach that takes into account the range of variability of mankind and avoids a simple reliance on averages or means. A consideration of variability and intermediates (the populationist approach) avoids the confusion that was faced by somatology in the early part of this century. At this point, after more than a hundred years of study, there are at least sixty systems for typing human body build, each probably equally valid. The number plus the limited explanatory power of such typologies has shown them to be more art than science. Each of the typing systems is successful only in emphasizing *differences*. In the long run, however, the striking feature of our species is the *similarities* between peoples—a condition which, because these similar peoples live in such diverse environments, requires careful study and explanation.

RACIAL BOUNDARIES: FACT OR FICTION

> . . . although there seems to be so great a difference between widely
> separate nations, that you might easily take the inhabitants of the
> Cape of Good Hope, the Greenlanders, and the Circassians for so
> many different species of man, yet when the matter is thoroughly considered, you see that all do so run into one another, and that one
> variety of mankind do so sensibly pass into the other that you cannot
> mark out the limits between them. [Blumenbach, 1770: 189, in J. S.
> Slotkin, ed., *Readings in Early Anthropology* (New York: Viking
> Fund Publications, 1965)]

Through overuse and vague application the term *race* has become so encumbered with contradictory and imprecise meanings that some workers now feel that it is useless. Many people take for granted that they know what "race" means and assume that scientific investigation has long ago proved the existence of significant human racial differences —yet, each time the term is applied, a definition must be provided so that the reader will know what concept it represents. There is even a considerable confusion over the number of divisions of mankind; as few as three and as many as thirty-seven races have been described. Two carefully written studies published in 1950 listed six and thirty races respectively (Boyd, 1950; Coon, Garn, and Birdsell, 1950).

Just what constitutes a race is a hard question to answer, since one's classification usually depends on the purpose of classification, and various approaches to taxonomy often have a built-in bias, especially when applied to man. It is usually assumed that there is an actual structure or collection of organisms in the natural world awaiting classification. The sample definitions that follow give some idea of the confusion surrounding the race concept in biology as well as anthropology.

Definitions of Race

DOBZHANSKY   Races are defined as populations differing in the incidence of certain genes, but actually exchanging or potentially able to exchange genes across whatever boundaries (usually geographic) separate them. (1944: 252)
Race differences are objectively ascertainable facts, the number of races we chose to recognize is a matter of convenience. (1962: 266)

HULSE   . . . races are populations which can be readily distinguished from one another on genetic grounds alone. (1963: 262)

BOYD   We may define a human race as a population which differs significantly from other human populations in regard to the frequency of one or more of the genes it possesses. It is an arbitrary matter which, and how many, gene loci we choose to consider as a significant "constellation". . . . (1950: 207)

GARN   At the present time there is general agreement that a race is a breeding population, largely if not entirely isolated reproductively from other breeding populations. The measure of race is thus reproductive isolation, arising commonly but not exclusively from geographical isolation. (1960: 7)

MAYR   A subspecies is an aggregate of local populations of a species, inhabiting a geographic subdivision of the range of the species, and differing taxonomically from other populations of the species. (1963: 348)

Because of the prejudice surrounding the concept of human races the following definition was offered, which substitutes *ethnic groups* for the term *race*.

MONTAGU   An ethnic group represents one of a number of populations, comprising the single species *Homo sapiens*, which individually maintain their differences, physical and cultural, by means of isolating mechanisms such as geographic and social barriers. These differences will vary as the power of the geographic and social barriers acting upon the original genetic differences varies. (1964: 317)

If these definitions are confusing and leave something to be desired, it may be because they avoid the chief question: "Why classify races of man?" It seems that classifications are continually being advanced because of the feeling that race is a real unit, even though classification schemes are impositions of arbitrary units on the natural world.[6] Also, the experience of the observer or classifier affects the way divisions are made, as noted by Boas over 35 years ago.

Actually the type of a population is always an abstraction of the striking peculiarities of the mass of individuals which are assumed to be represented combined in a single individual. What the striking peculiarities are depends largely upon the previous experiences of the observer, not upon the morphological value of the observed traits. This explains the diversities of opinion in taxonomic classification. (Boas, 1940: 173) [7]

The definitions above, though they appear quite diverse, have in common certain factors that they emphasize. The first is an assumption about the role of geographic distribution in race formation. Primarily, the divisions are based on the sharing of a common territory or point in space (see Figure 1-8). The second factor, all agree on the importance of breeding population in forming a collection of genes that sets the group apart. Beyond this there seems to be little agreement in terms of human racial divisions. In some opinions the division of mankind into racial groups distorts the facts and forces the investigator into erroneous channels of thinking. The two statements following illustrate this difference of opinion.

It is concluded that race may be defined operationally as a rough measure of genetic distance in human populations and as such may function as an informational construct in the multi-disciplinary area of research in human biology. (Paul T. Baker, 1967: 21)

[6] "To deny the existence of racial differences within the human species is futile. This futility has been neatly demonstrated at our symposium. I find it amusing that those who questioned the validity of racial classifications have themselves used the word 'race,' or the term 'so-called race,' many times. Indeed, how else could they speak about human variation at all! The reliability and the usefulness of racial classifications have often been exaggerated." T. Dobzhansky, *Science and the Concept of Race* (New York: Columbia University Press, 1968), pp. 166.

[7] The argument over the arbitrariness of racial taxonomies was carried on at some length in the last few years. See *Current Anthropology*, 3(3): 285–288, 1962.

FIGURE 1-8

(From Garn, 1961)

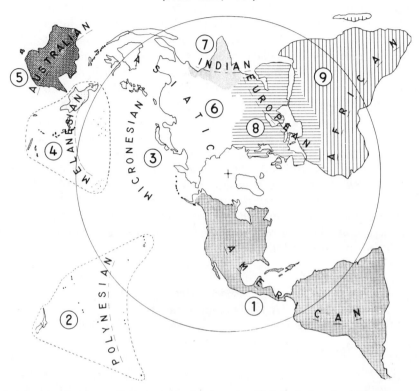

Polar-projection map of the world showing the limits of the nine geographical races described by Garn (1961). Geographical barriers set off the race-collections.

> Since races are open systems which are intergrading, the number of races will depend on the purpose of the classification . . . race isn't very important biologically. (S. L. Washburn, 1963: 524)

The contrasts between these definitions lead one to suspect that the authors may have had something different in mind when they used the term "race." Such a variation of meaning is one of the problems that has continually plagued anthropologists for generations in their attempt to study man. But, regardless of the numerous ways of looking at human diversity or the evaluation of the utility of race groupings, the fact remains that differences are real and cannot be either described or explained away by simple statements. The concept of race is not a taxonomic problem so much as a problem of the ways in which one views man in an evolutionary perspective.

By the end of the nineteenth century scientists began to appreciate that there was no single physical criterion for distinguishing between groups of mankind. However, it was believed that racial groupings could be delimited by association of several variables, and a number of writers proceeded to publish racial groupings which they believed to reflect the actual variability of our species. A casual survey shows that fourteen different race typologies have been described in this century. Most of them started with the major racial stocks defined earlier by Linneaus and Blumenbach, but they went further and subdivided each into several subgroups or local types.

This increase in subdivision illustrates the problem we often encounter in dealing with subspecies, either man or other mammals: the more we learn about the variability of the group, the more difficult it becomes to delimit them. As the numbers of races and local types of *H. sapiens* grew, the number of groupings was simply increased (see Tables 1-3a and b). Ripley, for example, in *The Races of Europe* (1899), decided that European populations consisted of three races: Nordic, Alpine, and Mediterranean. This concern with the identification of significant groups continued into the middle of the present century, when concern shifted

TABLE 1-3(a)

A Racial Classification [a]

(After C. S. Coon, S. Garn, and J. Birdsell, 1950, p. 140)

1. Murraylan	16. Hindu
2. Ainu	17. Mediterranean
3. Alpine	18. Nordic
4. N. W. European	19. N. American Colored
4a. N. W. European Prototype	20. S. African Colored
5. N. E. European	21. Classic Mongoloid
6. Lapp	22. N. Chinese
7. Forest Negro	23. S. E. Asiatic
8. Melanesian	24. Tibeto-Indonesian Mongoloid
9. Negrito	25. Turkic
10. Bushman	26. Am. Indian Marginal
11. Bantu	27. Am. Indian Central
12. Sundanese	28. Landino
13. Carpentarian	29. Polynesian
14. Dravidian	30. Neo-Hawaiian
15. Hamite	

[a]The authors described this classification as a tentative list. They stated: "The foregoing list of 30 'races' might have been ten or 50; the line of discrimination in many cases is arbitrary. In some cases we have nearly adequate data on which to base descriptions, in others almost none at all. . . . If this list does nothing else, we hope that it will bring home to the student the realization that race is not a static thing at all, but that new races are constantly being formed through the mechanisms described earlier in this Lecture, and that a new race such as the "Neo-Hawaiian" (#30) is just as real as an old one such as the Mediterranean (#17) or the Negrito (#9). History, in the biological as well as the cultural sense, is always in motion."

TABLE 1-3(b)

Major Racial Stocks

(After C. S. Coon, S. Garn, and J. Birdsell, 1950)

---

1. *Negroid:* All peoples showing special adaptation to bright light and intense heat, wherever found.
2. *Mongoloid:* The same for adaptation to intense cold.
3. *White:* Peoples of the Old World, excluding Australia and the southeastern fringe of Asia, who possess neither of these two kinds of adaptation. Overseas settlers of the same origin, and similar phenotypical form.
4. *Australoid:* The native inhabitants of Australia, whom one of us (Birdsell) has shown to belong to two distinct races and to include one other type. Veddas of Ceylon, and possibly some other remnant populations in Malaysia.
5. *American Indian:* The descendants of the pre-Columbian inhabitants of North, Central, and South America.
6. *Polynesian:* The inhabitants of the outer islands of the Pacific, from New Zealand to Hawaii to Easter Island. While moderately variable, they show resemblances to Mongoloids, White Australoids, and possibly Negroids.

---

toward the question of what race actually is. The following taxonomic schemes show this changing concern.

Earnest Hooton in *Up From The Ape* (1946) defined race as a group whose members present individually identical combinations of specific physical characters which they owe to their common descent. He divided man into three main physical groups or main races and subdivided these into an array of subcategories. His sorting criteria were primarily skin color, hair color, eye color, and hair form.

Coon, Garn, and Birdsell in *Races* (1950) described race as a population which differs phenotypically from all others. They distinguished six groups or "stocks" which grouped together thirty races. These races were determined on the basis of evolutionary status as reflected in certain features of the skull and body and special surface features, such as black skin and face form, which appear as special adaptations to the environment. In 1961 Garn offered a taxonomy of man differing somewhat from that constructed in his work with Birdsell and Coon. He described nine races, which were geographically delimited collections of local races. The local races were defined as breeding populations, the numbers of which in any geographical race were very large. A sample of thirty-two local races were listed as representative.

Boyd, in *Genetics and The Races of Man* (1950), defined six races on the basis of certain blood-type frequencies. By 1963 the distribution of the genes, which determine blood type, became better known, and Boyd increased his original six races to thirteen. The major increase was in the European group, from two to five. This expansion of the number of categories is clearly a result of the increased knowledge about blood types in the world's peoples (see Table 1-4).

TABLE 1-4

Racial Taxonomy of Homo Sapiens

Early Europeans		Early European
		Lapps
European		North West Europe
		Eastern Europe
		Mediterranean
African		African
Asiatic		Asian
		Indo-Dravidian
American Indian		American Indian
		Indonesian
		Melanesian
Australoid	Pacific	Polynesian
		Australoid

Carleton Coon described five groups of mankind in his *Origin of Races* (1962), in which he attempted to trace to mid-Pleistocene origins. These groups were referred to as subspecies, several of which were further divided—as in the case of Australoids, which consist of full-sized people and hereditary dwarfs (see Table 1-5). By a mixed criterion combining morphological traits (including skin color, blood type and fossilized skeletal remains) Coon was able to divide up *H. sapiens* into major racial stocks—mostly geographic races including a diversity of local races.

This geographic condition for man, the suiting of the race to its environment, was very early recognized. The gradation of skin color from the equator northward showed a concordant variation between pigmentation and latitude. Other characteristics, such as the "Mongoloid face" or stature, were quickly identified with a world region. These easily perceived characters have misled many investigators into stereotyping the world's populations. Often widely dispersed populations were placed into the same racial group; for example, all dark-skinned peoples were placed

TABLE 1-5

Classification of Modern Races

(After Carleton Coon, 1962, 1965)

Caucasoid		
Mongoloid		
Australoid		Negritos
		Full Sized
Congoid		Negroes
		Pygmies
Capoid		Bushmen
		Hottentots

in a category labeled Negroid. A commonly used distribution of human racial types is illustrated in Figure 1-8.

Similarities between groups, such as those shared by the dark-skinned peoples of Africa and parts of the Western Pacific (Melanesia), has been assumed to be due to close common ancestry. However, similarities as well as differences between human populations are actually due to a complex of factors; the mere sharing of a trait by two large segments of mankind does not demonstrate a close common ancestor a few generations back. Rather, the sharing of the traits is often due to factors in the environment that select for these characters.[8] Such a condition would also explain the range of variability, and the fact that when populations are better understood they appear to intergrade into one another, the previously supposed sharp boundaries disappearing.

Because of the nature of human reproduction each individual is unique, but in every population the individuals share numerous characteristics. Since the population (the basic breeding group within the species) is regionally defined, these characteristics appear as clusters in space; these clusters then often are identified as the basis for racial typologies. However, since the "typical" or "average" individual is an abstraction, a majority of a population covers a wide range of variation which overlaps with other groups, causing a gradient or cline of variation to be distributed over a wide area (see Figure 1-9). The concept of racial types has no significance in itself, and only under specified conditions are racial taxonomies useful to the zoologist.

The problem of studying man goes beyond the confusion over racial boundaries, however. Often the dilemma over taxonomy involves a question of human origins, especially the morphological appearance of certain racial groups. Early studies of human variability, particularly craniology, convinced many investigators that racial characters were permanent and not responsive to environmental influences. Numerous studies over the past generations have demonstrated just the opposite. The studies of Boas on immigrant populations in the United States proved that many cranial features (such as skull length and breadth as well as stature) were quite plastic and actually changed in one generation. For example, the children of immigrants from Eastern and Southern Europe were taller and larger with longer heads than their parents. These and other studies have shown that no single morphological character or even group of characteristics can be considered permanent and unchanging. This factor, by itself, makes the search for "pure" races in present or extinct populations a futile endeavor.

The collections or concentrations of characteristics that we see today

---

[8] See Ehrlich and Raven, "Differentiation of populations," *Science*, 165: 1228–1231, 1969.

FIGURE 1-9

Distribution of Human Skin Color

(From Brace and Montagu, 1965)

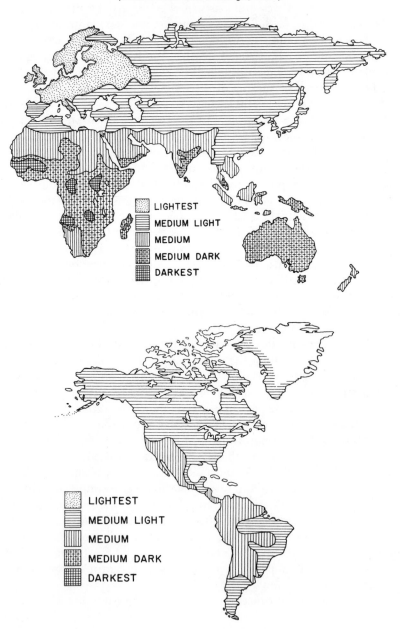

in certain regionally defined populations are probably the result of an ordering of genetic variability in response to the selective forces present in each environment. The history of populations is, of course, important, but the fossil record of man's past is not nearly complete enough to fill out an adequate record, nor are the total fossil remains of man's ancestors capable of establishing a record of unilineal evolution leading to any of the modern races. Some workers attempt to establish modern racial groupings in the fossil record of man's evolution. From this presumed evidence of racial origins they draw conclusions about the evolutionary position of modern groups. Regardless of what their race, subspecies, or stock is supposed to be, the fact is that all the varieties of living man can freely interbreed, as colonization, wars, and armies of occupation have clearly demonstrated during the last several hundred years.

Biological diversity is commonly associated with socially established categories, so that biological and cultural characteristics are often identified with one another. An example would be the treatment given the children of racially mixed marriages, who often are considered to possess traits or characteristics of behavior of the parent who is from the socially disadvantaged group [such as Negro, Indian, or Aborigine (Australian)]. This "phenotypic imagery" leads to assumptions that behavior is related closely to biological group affinity and that racial differences are essential to understanding human behavior. It is the confusion of levels of abstraction (the mixing of the biologically determined with the socially acquired traits) that makes studies of *H. sapiens* so difficult. True, the evolution of man can be understood only as a mixture of social biological phenomena, but man's biological makeup is largely inherited, while his behavior is mainly the result of the experiences, the conditioning he undergoes within his social group. To confuse the two or to freely interchange them is tantamount to saying that the Navahos or Eskimos speak in their respective languages because of their genetic inheritance.

All of the groupings listed above have a geographical basis for their racial divisions, which should not be surprising, since geography helps establish the forces of natural selection that act on our species. Man's variability is often distributed in a geographical pattern. Throughout the book we shall carefully consider geographic influences, especially in the action of natural selection on the populations.

What, then, is the origin of human diversity? If race or subspecies is an artificial construct—a device of convenience to enable man's mind to organize information from the natural world—then origins cease to be an important consideration. Rather our concern should be with the possible responses to the environment that our species is capable of biologically. With this in mind, we will attempt to sort out the different influences on *Homo sapiens*. Race, group, or population will be used to refer to that geographically and culturally determined collection of individuals who share in a common gene pool.

RECOMMENDED READINGS AND
LITERATURE CITED

BAKER, PAUL T. 1967. "The biological race concept as a research tool," *Am. J. Phys. Anthrop.*, 27: 21–25.

BARZUN, JACQUES. 1965. *Race: A Study in Superstition*. New York: Harper & Row.

BOAS, FRANZ. 1940. "The relations between physical and social anthropology," in *Race, Language and Culture*. New York: The Free Press.

BOYD, W. C. 1950. *Genetics and the Races of Man*. Boston: Little, Brown & Co.

COON, C. S. 1962. *The Origin of Races*. New York: Alfred A. Knopf.

COON, C. S., S. M. GARN, and J. B. BIRDSELL. 1950. *Races: A Study of the Problems of Race Formation in Man*. Springfield, Ill.: Charles C Thomas.

DARLINGTON, C. D. 1947. "The genetic component of language," *Heredity*, 1: 269–286.

DOBZHANSKY, T. 1944. "On species and races of living and fossil man," *Am. J. Phys. Anthrop.*, 2: 251–265.

———. 1962. *Mankind Evolving: The Evolution of the Human Species*. New Haven and London: Yale University Press.

———. 1968. *Science and the Concept of Race*. New York: Columbia University Press.

EHRLICH, PAUL R., and PETER H. RAVEN. 1969. "Differentiation of population," *Science*, 165: 1228–1232.

GARN, STANLEY M., ed. 1960. *Readings on Race*. Springfield, Ill.: Charles C Thomas.

———. 1961. *Human Races*. Springfield Ill.: Charles C Thomas.

HOOTON, EARNEST A. 1946. *Up From The Ape*. New York: Macmillan.

HULSE, FREDERICK S. 1963. *The Human Species*. New York: Random House.

MAYR, ERNST. 1963. *Animal Species and Evolution*. Cambridge, Mass.: The Belknap Press of Harvard University.

MONTAGU, ASHLEY. 1964. "Discussion and criticism on the race concept," *Current Anthrop.*, 5: 317.

MORTON, S. G. 1839. *Crania Americana*. Philadelphia: J. Dodson.

NASH, MANNING. 1962. "Race and the ideology of race," *Current Anthrop.*, 3: 285–288.

PUTNAM, CARLETON. 1967. *Race and Reality*. Washington, D.C.: Public Affairs Press.

RIPLEY, W. Z. 1899. *The Races of Europe*. New York: Appleton.

SLOTKIN, J. S., ed. 1965. *Readings in Early Anthropology*. New York: Viking Fund Publications.

STANTON, W. R. 1960. *The Leopard's Spots: Scientific Attitudes Toward Race in America, 1815–59*. Chicago: University of Chicago Press.

WASHBURN, S. L. 1963. "The study of race," *American Anthrop.*, 65: 521–531.

chapter two

The Biological
Basis
for
Human Variation

Man shares modes of reproduction with most of the other mammals, and inheritance mechanisms are the same. These mechanisms of inheritance are the source of much of the vast diversity seen in the biological world, which, though it may at times seem to be extremely random and unfettered, is in fact subject to limits on the extent and degree of variation in each species. *H. sapiens,* the species we are most concerned with, contains as much or perhaps more variation than any other mammalian group, but its diversity is limited in certain unique ways.

PRINCIPLES OF INHERITANCE

Parents' characteristics are passed along to offspring in the form of biochemical units called genes. Through combinations of these units the basic plan for the adult form is established, and as the individual grows these genetic units regulate the growth and development process. Ultimately, in conjunction with the environment, the genes determine the individual's appearance and range of responses to various stimuli from the environment.

The mode of inheritance, as well as the various gene combinations and ratios, have been worked out quite carefully since Mendel's original experiments.[1] Though man is a complicated organism with a long life-span and perhaps tens of thousands of gene units, certain of his characteristics have been related to a series of simple gene combinations, and a number of human traits are known to be inherited in particular ways which can be predicted with a high degree of accuracy.

Dominant Inheritance

Some traits are inherited as dominants; the presence of a single dominant gene will cause the trait to be expressed. If one parent has a trait determined by a dominant gene, there is a 50 percent chance that the children will possess it. *Chondrodystrophy*, a type of human dwarfism, occurs when a person possesses the mutant gene for his condition; malformation of the long bones of the body will cause the individual to be much shorter than normal. If a chondrodystrophic dwarf marries a normal person, each child they produce will have a 50 percent chance of possessing this affliction.

Another well-known affliction, the famous *Hapsburg lip*, is also de-

---

[1] THE FOUNDER OF GENETICS: JOHANN GREGOR MENDEL *(1822–1884)*. A lengthy series of experiments performed in the mid-nineteenth century provided the basis for the science of genetics. These experiments were carried out on several common varieties of garden plants by Johann Gregor Mendel, who was studying plant hybridization. He concentrated much of his efforts on the sweet pea and showed, by multiple crosses, that several traits were inherited as discrete units, not as a blending of parental characteristics as was generally believed at the time.

Plants with yellow seeds were crossed with green-seeded ones, and the result was a generation of plants which produced only yellow seeds. When plants from this generation were crossed, a mixture of yellow-seeded and green-seeded plants were produced. Similar results were obtained when plants were selected for seed shape. Plants with smooth seeds were crossed with wrinkled-seeded plants, yielding only plants with smooth seeds. These results led Mendel to advance the basic law of *segregation*. He explained that the trait, which we now call a phenotype, was due to paired factors or hereditary units (these units became known as genes in 1909). Some factors were dominant to others and, further, each segregated independently of the other in the next generation.

Mendel extended his experiments to include crosses for two characteristics at a time. Smooth yellow-seeded plants were crossed with wrinkled green-seeded ones. The results of these crosses are illustrated in Figure 2-1. Through these series of crosses Mendel found that the heredity factors of each trait were separate and would assort independently.

We can appreciate the mathematical implication of Mendel's experiments in terms of the *Mendelian ratio*. Mendel produced a quantification of his results so that the number of plants with certain traits in each generation could be (probabilistically) predicted—a capability which has proved vital in modern population genetics.

Mendel's experiments, though not appreciated at the time, provided a correct insight into inheritance opposed to the then current belief of inheritance by blending. His *particulate* inheritance theory, together with the laws of segregation and independent assortment, provides a foundation for modern genetics.

termined by a dominant gene. Individuals with this condition have a protruding lower jaw and enlarged lower lip, and chances are that half of their children will show the same abnormality. A white streak or forelock in the hair is also the result of the action of a dominant gene. These simple dominants fully express their characteristics each generation, and a simple ratio or proportion exists; if one parent has the trait, there is a 50 percent chance that each child conceived will also possess it. However, if both parents have the trait, then the probability that their children will have it increases to three-fourths.

Recessive Inheritance

Unlike simple dominant genes, recessives sometimes cause characteristics to appear in children of unafflicted parents, often to their dismay. Rather than blame one's grandparents or argue that devilish forces are at work, it is best to recognize that man possesses many genes whose actions or potential actions are masked by the expression of the more dominant form. Such genes, called *recessives,* can cause a characteristic to appear in an individual only when they combine as a pair (homozygous combination). A number of human traits are determined in this way.

An example is a well-known condition which interrupts the synthesis of the pigment melanin and causes the individual to be without color in his hair and skin; such an individual is known as an albino. This condition occurs in European populations only about once in twenty thousand births, but once in three thousand births in several Nigerian populations. In a majority of these cases the parents were normal but each possessed the recessive gene for albinism; these genes combined upon conception to produce an offspring who had the recessive pair. A similar condition occurs in the ABO blood group system. The gene that determines type O blood is recessive to both the A gene and the B gene. Hence it often occurs that parents, neither of whom is type O, have an offspring with type O blood. This indicates that the parents were carrying the type O gene, which was recessive and hence masked by the action of either the A or the B gene.

The ratio of recessive-trait occurrence in each generation depends upon the gene combinations of the parents and is somewhat more difficult to determine than the simple dominant ratio. If neither parent has the trait but both are carriers of the recessive gene, there is a 25 percent chance that a child they produce will have the recessive trait. But if one parent is the carrier and the other parent has the trait, then there is a 50 percent chance that their child will have the condition.

FIGURE 2-1a
Genotypic Model

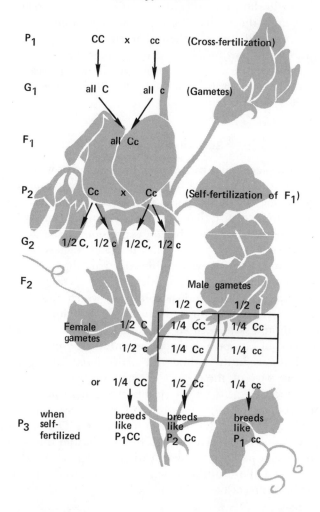

P_1	CC x cc	(Cross-fertilization)	
G_1	all C all c	(Gametes)	
F_1	all Cc		
P_2	Cc x Cc	(Self-fertilization of F_1)	
G_2	1/2 C, 1/2 c 1/2 C, 1/2 c		

F_2

Male gametes

		1/2 C	1/2 c
Female gametes	1/2 C	1/4 CC	1/4 Cc
	1/2 c	1/4 Cc	1/4 cc

or   1/4 CC   1/2 Cc   1/4 cc

P_3 when self-fertilized

breeds like P_1CC   breeds like P_2 Cc   breeds like P_1 cc

Genotypic Model proposed to explain phenotypic results of certain crosses involving colored and colorless pea plants. (From I. H. Herskowitz, "Genetics," Little, Brown and Co., 1962. Reprinted by permission of I. H. Herskowitz.)

Mendelian Ratios

The examples above show how inheritance can be predicted in the cases of simple dominant and recessive genes. Inheritance is regular, no generations are skipped, and the traits are easily identified. These con-

FIGURE 2-1b
Phenotypic Results

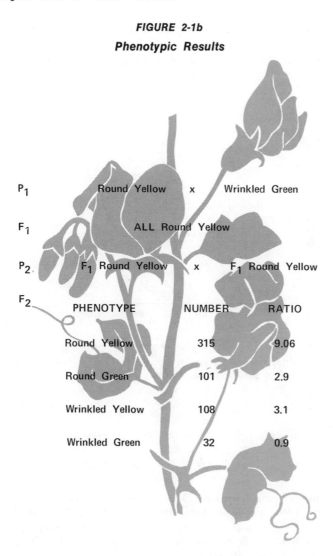

P_1 Round Yellow   x   Wrinkled Green

F_1 ALL Round Yellow

P_2 F_1 Round Yellow   x F_1 Round Yellow

F_2

PHENOTYPE	NUMBER	RATIO
Round Yellow	315	9.06
Round Green	101	2.9
Wrinkled Yellow	108	3.1
Wrinkled Green	32	0.9

Phenotypic results from studying two traits simultaneously.
(From I. H. Herskowitz, "Genetics," Little, Brown and Co.,
1962. Reprinted by permission of I. H. Herskowitz.)

ditions, unfortunately, do not exist for the majority of man's genes, and
expressions of genetically determined conditions are much more complicated—but the inheritance mechanisms and predictability remain the
same. It is just more difficult to determine the presence or absence of some
genes. These kinds of gene combinations will be discussed further on. At

this point we consider some examples of dominant and recessive genes.

If "A" is used to represent a dominant gene and small "a" to represent the recessive, then the following probabilistic ratios prevail:

1. If one parent has the dominant gene:

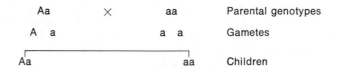

The probability is that 50 percent of the children will carry the dominant gene.

2. If both parents are carriers of the dominant gene:

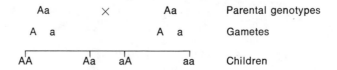

There is a probability that 75 percent will be carriers.

3. If both parents are carriers of a recessive, as in the case of type O gene, the following ratios will be possible:

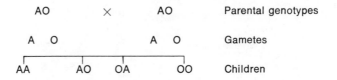

This diagram shows that 75 percent of the children will probably be type A (the type of the dominant gene) and 25 percent will be type O.

4. If a person who is a carrier of the type O gene marries a person with type O blood (a person who possesses a pair of type O genes), the following ratio will result:

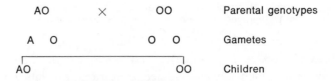

5. However, if a person who has type O blood mates with a person who is type A, but who is not a carrier of the recessive, the following ratio can exist:

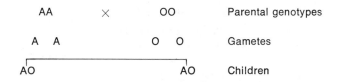

All offspring will be type A but will be carriers of the recessive.

MECHANISMS OF INHERITANCE

In the examples of inheritance just given, each characteristic was shown as a result of a paired combination of genes which occurred in predictable ratios from generation to generation. We shall now consider the mode of transmission and the way in which genes are combined to form the elemental structure of the new individual.

Chromosomes

The genes are carried within the body cells by threadlike structures known as chromosomes, which reside within the nucleus of each cell during the major part of the cell's life cycle. The number of chromosomes is fixed for each species; man has 46, while the chimp and gorilla have 48 and the gibbon 44. The 46 chromosomes in man are arranged as 23 pairs, of which 22 are known as autosomes and one as the sex chromosomes, since they are responsible for sex determination. Structural uniqueness sets the autosomes apart and prevents, except in unusual circumstances, a combination of chromosomes from different pairs.

Since the number of chromsomes is critical and must remain constant from one generation to the next, the basic problem is how to pass on the hereditary material carried by the chromosomes in equal amounts to the next generation. Because sexual reproduction involves the combining of materials from two individuals to produce the offspring, this problem of maintenance of chromosome number is solved by a process of reduction and division known as meiosis. *Meiosis* is to a certain extent, comparable to *mitosis* of somatic cell division, with several important exceptions (see Figure 2-2). The major distinction is one of number: the dividing cell must double the number of chromosomes shortly before division, as in mitosis, while production of special cells called *gametes* must cause the chromosome number to be halved upon final division.

The germ cells are formed in specialized tissues found in the gonads whose major function is production of the gametes—eggs in the case of a female and sperm in the case of a male. These cells undergo meiosis, which divides the chromosome pairs to form a gamete able to combine

FIGURE 2-2

Stages of Cell Division

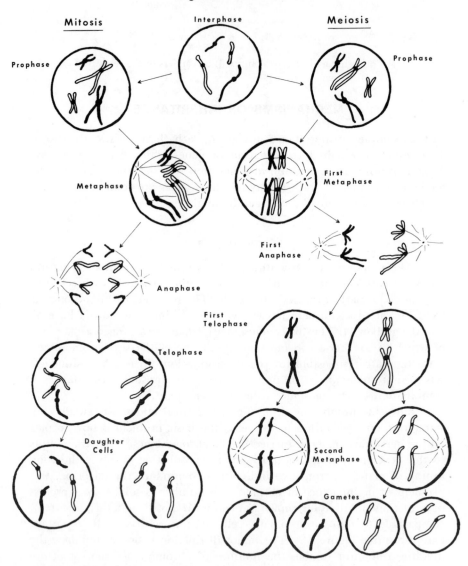

with a gamete of the opposite sex in order to form the fertilized egg or
zygote. This fertilized egg combines chromosomes from each parent in
order to duplicate the proper number of chromosomes for the species.
This process of sexual reproduction is one of the most fundamental and
important factors for the introduction of variation, since it combines

materials from two individuals. Variation also may be introduced during meiosis by the crossing over of parts from homologous chromosomes during certain stages of chromosome replication (see Figure 2-6).

The Gene

Each gene has a particular place along the chromosome structure where it is normally located. This position or *locus* will be available for the gene on each chromosome of a pair. Each of the loci along the chromosome has a special relationship to certain characteristics—for example, a locus for an enzyme, blood type, or hemoglobin. The way in which the character is determined depends on the gene that is present at the locus. In the case of albinism, if the dominant gene is present, then the individual will have normal skin pigmentation, but if the recessive gene is present on both loci of the chromosome pair then the individual will lack pigmentation. These genes, or any genes that are related because they can occur at a locus for a particular characteristic, are known as *alleles* or alternate genetic forms.

Many if not most loci on man's chromosomes have several alleles which contribute to the wide range of variability. The presence of two or more alleles at a locus, neither being rare, is known as *polymorphism.* Another way of describing this concept is to consider the simultaneous presence of alternate forms of a gene (alleles) within the same population, none of the alleles occurring at less than one percent. Hence, man is polymorphic for several blood groups, for hemoglobin, taste sensitivity (PTC), and many other traits.

Since chromosomes are present as paired structures during meiosis, a locus on one chromosome will have a locus on the opposite chromosome except in the special case of the sex chromosomes. The autosomal genes will always exist in pairs, and this pair, called the *genotype,* determines the potential response of the individual to his environment. The interaction between the genotype and the environment results in a characteristic that is identifiable and is variable, with a few exceptions, over a wide range. Such a characteristic is called the *phenotype.* Body size, though coded by a number of gene pairs, could be used as an example; the potential for growth is determined by the genotypes a person possesses, and the ultimate size achieved depends upon the environment during growth and development. A person raised on a starvation diet will not achieve his full growth or realize his maximum body-size potential. Skin color, another phenotype, is the result of the interaction of several genotypes. The degree of a person's skin coloration is due to the interaction of these gene products and solar radiation in the ultraviolet range.

Gene Action

The gene can be thought of as a code which stores information needed by the organism for proper growth and development as well as for regulation of metabolic functions. This code has been described as a *DNA* molecule, which, by its structure, can provide information that will enable the cells of the body to function properly and to divide when necessary. These processes are based on the DNA structure's capacity to direct the synthesis of strings of amino acids to form protein in the cell (see Figure 2-3). The resulting protein may be used to rebuild tissue such as skin, blood, or bone, or it may be an enzyme that regulates biochemical processes in the body.

DNA functions as an information storage mechanism for the next generation, and the molecule must be replicated faithfully during each successive step of cell division so that the daughter cells can function properly. Sometimes an error occurs; the result is an important change of code in the new cell. This mistake in duplication of the DNA sequence is known as a *mutation*. If the mutation occurs in a body cell during mitosis,

FIGURE 2-3

The Four-Stage Process of Assembly of a Polypeptide Chain

(From Marshall W. Nirenberg, "The Genetic Code: II," © 1963 by Scientific American, Inc., All Rights Reserved.)

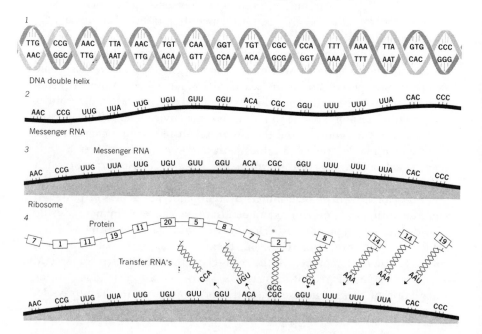

the result will not be passed on to the next generation but will remain in the individual's somatic cells. However, if an error or mutation occurs during meiosis, when gametes are formed, this genetic mistake can be transmitted when reproduction takes place. There is a chance that gene mutants will be passed on from one generation to the next, but mutations of genes take place at very low rates in man and they cannot be predicted. They occur randomly, although exposure to X rays or other sources of ionizing radiation seems to hasten the process.

Mutations, although usually detrimental, are important in introducing new genetic forms into a population, increasing the number of alleles at the different loci. Therefore mutations are the ultimate source of variability of a species, and, as such, are the foundation for the wide diversity we see in the biological world. (Table 2-1 gives several mutation rates in man.)

TABLE 2-1
Human Mutation Rates for Several Traits

Trait	Population	Mutations per Million Gametes
Autosomal Dominants		
Retinoblastoma, an eye tumor	—	15–23
Chondrodystrophy, dwarfism	Denmark	43
Chondrodystrophy, dwarfism	Sweden	70
Retinoblastoma	England	14
Retinoblastoma	Michigan	23
Palmaris longus muscle	United States (whites)	32
Palmaris longus muscle	United States (Negroes)	7
Huntington's chorea (involuntary uncontrollable movements)	United States (whites)	5.4
Autosomal Recessives		
Infantile amaurotic idiocy, (Tay-Sachs disease)	Eastern European Jews	38
Albinism	United States (whites)	28
Albinism	Japan	28
Infantile amaurotic idiocy	Japan	11
Cystic fibrosis of pancreas	—	0.7–1.0
Phenylketonuria	United States (whites)	25
Sex Linked		
Hemophilia	—	25–32
Muscular dystrophy	—	43–100
Hemophilia	England	20
Hemophilia	Denmark	32

The Sex Chromosomes

The sex of an individual is determined by a combination of the X and Y chromosomes; if two X chromosomes are combined, the individual will be a female, but if an X is combined with a Y, he will be male. Any deviation from these two combinations yields an individual with many abnormal characteristics. Occasionally (about once in every four hundred male births) an extra X chromosome is combined with the XY pair; the offspring will be a male with poorly developed sexual characteristics and some female ones (*Klinefelter Syndrome*). If a female lacks an X chromosome (which occurs once in every three thousand five hundred female births), she will have a series of anatomical defects known as the *Turner*

FIGURE 2-4

Chromosomes in Mitosis
(From McKusick, 1969)

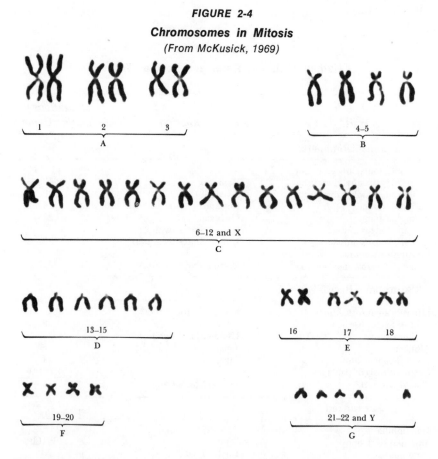

The mitotic metaphase chromosomes of a somatic cell of a male, arranged in a karyotype.

Syndrome, and the diploid number will be 45 instead of the normal 46. Recently, males with the XYY condition have been discovered. They are taller than the average male, and there are claims that they are more aggressive in their behavior, sometimes showing antisocial tendencies. Recent studies, however, question the interrelationship between the extra Y chromosome and behavior. The most conservative conclusion now is that association is not clear.

The major significance of the X and Y chromosomes aside from sex determination is that the Y differs considerably in structure from the X. It is shorter, so that a region of the X is not represented by a corresponding region of the Y (Figure 2-4). Any genes appearing on the *nonhomologous* region of the X chromosome will not be paired up in male cells. Therefore, a certain number of genes on the nonhomologous region of the X chromosome will be expressing their product without any influence from other alleles. This fact leads to the existence of certain recessive traits in our species that occur more frequently in the hemizygous male then in the female.

Usually, these X-linked traits are caused by recessive genes. Since they are frequently paired with a normal dominant in the female, because she has two X chromosomes, they rarely occur in women. Some of the better-known traits are *hemophilia, red-green colorblindness,* and *G6PD deficiency,* which are due to recessive genes inherited as shown in the diagram (Figure 2-5).

Little is known about Y-chromosome influence on inheritance in the male, but the genes on this chromosome do in some way seem to influence the development of male characteristics. An individual without the Y chromosome, X0 or XX, will be a female. The Y-linked genes determine traits that influence growth and development to the extent that the sexes are dimorphic, with the male tending to be larger and to have more body hair and a beard.

Gene Combinations and Interactions

The inheritance of many characteristics is complicated by the influence of elements in addition to the single gene pair. Skin color is one such trait. Though a single gene can cause a lack of skin pigmentation, as in albinism, the condition is inherited as a combination of genes. The effect of this multiple gene combination on a single trait is called *polygenic* inheritance. In addition, certain genes influence the development of more than one phenotype, as in the case of phenylketonuria; such genes are called *pleiotropic.* Persons with this condition are unable to metabolize properly the amino acid phenylalanine, so that large amounts accumulate in the blood together with phenylpyruvic acid, an alternate product (see

FIGURE 2-5

An Example of X-Linked Traits: Red-Green Colorblindness

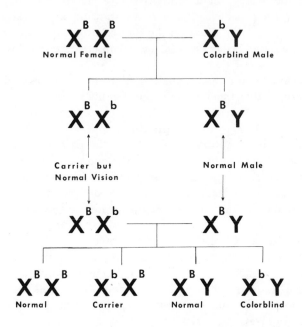

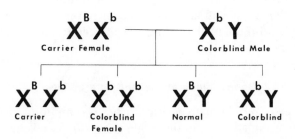

page 85). This condition, inherited as a single rare recessive allele, results not only in improper use of the amino acid but a disturbance of pigment formation and impairment of the development of the central nervous system, so the individual will be mentally retarded. Polygenic characters also frequently have pleiotropic effects. The development of the nasal region, for example, appears to be closely correlated with the position

and size of the roots of the canine teeth, whose tips are placed very close to the borders of the nasal aperture. The genes that control one structure probably control an adjacent closely related structure—in this case the nasal region of the face and the canine teeth.

Genes do not always cause a character to be expressed in the same way, and sometimes the phenotype does not appear at all, even though the genotype for it is present. This results in the skipping of generations, which occurs when the gene is partly *penetrant*. In some individuals autosomal dominant traits may be more severe then in other persons. This condition, known as variable *expressivity*, is illustrated by the presence of extra fingers or toes (*polydactyly*). A dominant gene causes the presence of extra fingers or toes, but the gene is not always expressed in the same way. Sometimes an extra digit will appear on the hands or feet, or sometimes only a single extra digit will be present.

BIOLOGICAL UNITS

We have been discussing the mechanisms of inheritance and the effects of genes on individuals; now we must consider the groups or units within which individuals interact. These are the groups or units that evolution acts on and that alter their composition through time in response to the forces of the environment. The group contains a certain range of variability in many characteristics, but the most favorable traits are in the majority. We shall be concerned with the variation and distribution of traits as well as the group's actions that enable the establishment of the next generation.

Species refers to a group or collection of populations who share a large number of characteristics. Interbreeding takes place exclusively within the species; therefore "a large group of organisms reproductively isolated from other such groups" is a way of defining species. By this criterion a species is a real taxonomic unit.

The venerable idea of species is based on observation of the striking discontinuity of life forms in nature. The study of this discontinuity between living organisms developed into a field of study which recognized a species as something "different" and used these differences to group animals in the natural world. The appraisal, based on morphological traits, did not take into account the range of variability and therefore was often misleading, as in the case of a polytypic species. This older typological approach has been replaced in biology by the recognition of the great diversity in many species and an awareness that the type or average is an abstraction.

Population

The variation in a species is often grouped according to geographical region. A species often is spread over broad areas in a series of geographically defined groups. The polytypic condition is especially apparent in man, who has been able to adapt to a wide variety of environments. A group of individuals who are potentially interbreeding, who occupy a local area, and who make up a basic breeding unit of our species is called a *breeding population* or sometimes a *deme*. It is the unit that evolution acts on, and its genetic composition is the result of several interacting factors in the environment which tend to limit variability to a specific range. The breeding population, then, consists of a number of individuals who possess a large number of characteristics in common, though there is a degree of variation.

Within each population the gene combinations are reassorted each generation through the mechanisms involved in the reproduction process. The total number of combinations of all genes provides a *gene pool,* whose composition natural forces may alter each generation. The distribution of characteristics determined by the gene frequencies within this group may be described by a normal curve, as in the case of stature or skin color. This concept of gene pool contrasts to the idea of type or average, which emphasizes the central tendency (or mean) and ignores or tends to diminish the significance of the range of variation. Typological comparisons of groupings of individuals or populations throughout the species tends to emphasize means, stressing differences between one type and another—whereas in reality there is a great deal of similarity between widely disbursed populations within our species. The *populationist* view considers the distribution of traits throughout the gene pool and attempts to show the similarity between adjacent populations, which could be illustrated by the wide range of overlap of these normal curves of a population. Geographical distributions of many gene frequencies form a continuum over a wide area, the gene frequencies of each population overlapping those of its neighbors. The effect can be a smooth *clinal* distribution of gene frequencies.

FACTORS OF VARIATION AND EVOLUTION

Evolution has been described as *descent with modification,* a definition which refers to alteration of organisms throughout thousands of generations. It works well with studies of species over long periods, as in the evolution of the primates (see Figure 1-7). Many modifications can be seen when comparisons are made between living representatives and their extinct ancestors. Smaller, more subtle changes occur within modern populations—perhaps only a slight alteration in the frequency of occurrence of certain genes. This, too, is evolution, though some writers differentiate by calling changes in gene frequency between generations *microevolution*. A broader definition of evolution, then, is *change in gene frequency through time*.

Sources of Variation

Stability and change within a biological unit (or gene pool) depend upon a great many factors. If these factors balance out so that a net change takes place from one generation to the next, the result is evolution. If the elements that cause change are counteracted by those that tend to maintain stability, then there will be no change in gene pool composition. Such stability is, of course, an ideal situation. The actual condition of a population is a small variation from generation to generation. Only when this variation becomes directional does evolution take place.

Mutation—The ultimate source of all genetic variability is mutation, which can be described simply as a change in the genetic code. The simplest type involves an alteration of a single nucleotide base (see Figure 2-3), often called a *point mutation*. Other types are alterations in the lineal sequence of genes on the chromosomes themselves.

The point mutation is believed to be the most important type since it actually introduces new genetic information into the gene pool. New alleles are formed in this way, and the multiple alleles at most of the loci on the chromosomes are the raw material on which evolution can work.

Recombination—During meiosis each chromosome segregates independently; therefore, chromosomes that are provided the individual at conception by the gamete from the male parent or the female parent often are separated (see Figure 2-2). This is one type of recombination, demonstrating how different types of gametes can be produced. The total number of gamete types (with different groups of chromosomes) that can be produced by *H. sapiens* is 2^{23}.

A second type of recombination that occurs during meiosis is *crossover*. Crossover refers to exchange between homologous chromosomes of part of their structure. This causes a realignment of the linear arrangement of genes along the chromosome, and the frequency of this occurrence or the chance that it will happen depends upon the distance between the genes (see Figure 2-6).

Unlike mutation, recombination does not insert new information into the gene pool. It merely reassorts the already existing genes so that individuals in the new generation will have different gene arrangements.

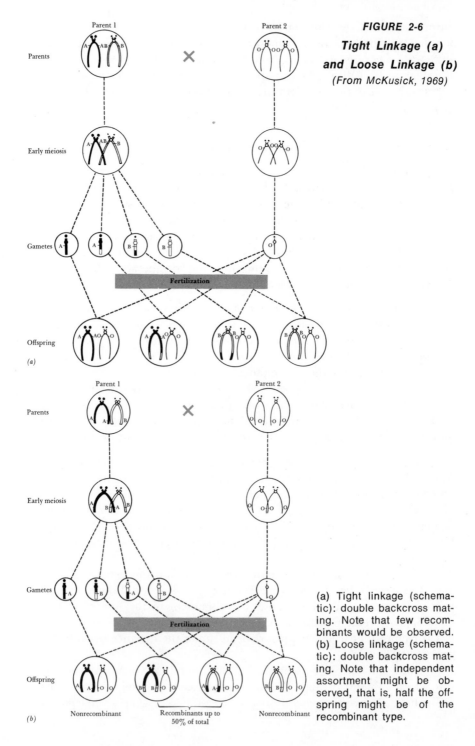

FIGURE 2-6

Tight Linkage (a)
and Loose Linkage (b)
(From McKusick, 1969)

(a) Tight linkage (schematic): double backcross mating. Note that few recombinants would be observed.
(b) Loose linkage (schematic): double backcross mating. Note that independent assortment might be observed, that is, half the offspring might be of the recombinant type.

Since these gene arrangements or genotypes, discussed earlier, determine the characteristics, *recombination* is an important source of variability within the gene pool.

Gene Flow—Throughout human history a great deal of population movement has taken place. With this migration and mixing of peoples an increased genetic exchange has occurred. Interpopulation contact, as through trade and warfare, has also caused gene exchange between populations' gene pools. These forms of genetic exchange result in an increased variability of the gene pool; we shall call them *gene flow*.

Gene flow—the force opposed to influences of population isolation—prevents the development of unique genetic combinations in a gene pool but has the potential for introducing new gene combinations into the pool.

Population Size—Population size is also a critical factor. When the population is very small there is a likelihood that certain gene combinations will not be represented in the next generation. This can be compared to a sampling error. When a sample is taken of a population, the smaller the sample the less likely it is that the sample will be representative of the whole. The same applies to reproduction of the next generation.[2]

An example of this phenomenon [3] is the case of the Dunkers, a religious isolate in Pennsylvania. This group consists of approximately 300 persons, the descendants of a colony founded in the nineteenth century by German Baptist Brethren. In 1952 Glass and his co-workers made an extensive genetic study and found that the Dunkers differed significantly in certain gene frequencies from the average in United States populations and also from populations in Germany, from which the group's ancestors migrated. Major differences were seen in blood type A and O, where type A increased and O decreased. The implications of these changes will be considered in Chapter 4.

Founder's principle is often confused with genetic drift.[4] In a way it, too, is a sampling error, since it is improbable that a small group of colonists will be representative of a cross section of the parent population. The migrants who land on uninhabited islands and establish ongoing populations probably do not contain all the genotypes present in the gene pool from which they came; as an example one could consider Pitcairn's Island, Tristan Da Cuna, or, in more ancient times, the Hawaiian Islands. Also, sampling errors probably occurred in the many religious groups that migrated to the United States, as with the Dunkers. The Hutterites of

[2] In some groups the effective breeding population is small, and frequently a minority of females reproduce a majority of children.

[3] Sometimes called the *Sewall Wright effect* or *genetic drift*.

[4] First proposed by Ernst Mayr to describe the effect on a new population founded by a small number of colonists (see Mayr, 1963: 211).

North Dakota and Saskatchewan, who today consist of over 10,000 individuals, are descendants of about 90 founders. A factor that often helps restrict the variety of genotypes represented is that the migrants frequently are composed of many members of the same family lineage. This was noted by Neel and Salzano (1964), when they observed that closely related villages of South American Indians (Yanomama) differed in gene frequencies. The differences are probably due to the practice of splitting along family lines when new villages were established, producing the "lineal effect."

Forces for Stability

Although there is a strong and apparently random tendency for a population to vary, nonetheless not all combinations in genotypes and their resultant characteristics exist. Any survey of a population's diversity shows that there are limits to the range, and that certain traits occur more frequently than others. Forces for stability oppose the forces for variation, so that population range and diversity approximate the normal curve.

Natural Selection—In each breeding population some organisms— because of their genetic complement—reproduce at a great rate. Therefore, there will be a disproportionate representation of their genotypes in the next generation. These groups, by definition, are the most fit individuals in the population and might be described as those that are being selectedly favored.[5] Those individuals who produce less frequently are therefore less fit. These conditions lead to a reduction in variation.

The sum total of all of these conditions may be referred to as *natural selection*. All factors that reduce the individual's capacity to pass on genes to future generations are included. Factors that reduce reproductive lifespan, such as disease or predation, are examples if certain segments of a population are more susceptible to them. In short, natural selection is differential reproduction (several examples of selection in man will be provided in later chapters).

In man the effects of natural selection are complicated by many aspects of human behavior. One that acts as an antivariation force is preferential mating. In all human societies certain individuals are more likely to mate because of society's rules and because of concepts of what is desirable (the ideals of beauty, social class, economic circumstances, and so on). This *nonrandom* mating reduces the chance combination of genes and further restricts or limits the range of diversity in any human gene pool.

---

[5] The fitness of an individual is measured in terms of his or her reproductive success or *Darwinian fitness*.

Population Equilibrium—If the factors that introduce population variability are counteracted by forces for stability, the population will be in equilibrium and gene frequencies will remain the same from generation to generation. This fact is now well understood. At the beginning of the twentieth century, however, the general idea about genetics was that the dominant allele would overcome the recessive and eventually would be the only allele for the locus. In other words, the dominant gene would have a swamping effect, and the percentage of the recessive allele in the population would decline and eventually disappear.

In 1908 two scientists independently developed a mathematical concept of the relationship between a pair of allelic genes which showed that, under certain conditions, there would be no change in gene frequency. This *Hardy-Weinberg equilibrium* is written as

$$p + q = 1.$$

Simply stated, it means that if one allele increases, the other decreases. The equation for the genotype frequencies would be

$$p^2 + 2pq + q^2 = 1$$

or, substituting the genotype symbols,

$$AA + 2Aa + aa = 1.$$

No matter what the original frequency of alleles A and a, the genotypes would remain in this ratio.[6]

[6] McKusick (1969) offers the following details:

Parents		Frequency of Mating	Frequency of offspring [a]			Numerical example		
Male	Female		AA	Aa	aa	AA	Aa	aa
AA x AA		p^4	p^4	—	—	6,561	0	0
AA x Aa Aa x AA		$4p^3q$	$2p^3q$	$2p^3q$	—	1,458	1,458	0
AA x aa aa x AA		$2p^2q^2$	—	$2p^2q^2$	—	0	162	0
Aa x Aa		$4p^2q^2$	p^2q^2	$2p^2q^2$	p^2q^2	81	162	81
Aa x aa aa x Aa		$4pq^3$	—	$2pq^3$	$2pq^3$	0	18	18
aa x aa		q^4	—	—	q^4	0	0	1
All types		1	p^2	$2pq$	q^2	8,100	1,800	100

[a] The AA column adds up to $p^4 + 2p^3q + p^2q^2$, or $p^2(p^2 + 2pq + q^2)$, or p^2.
The Aa column adds up to $2p^3q + 4p^2q^2 + 2pq^3$, or $2pq(p^2 + 2pq + q^2)$, or $2pq$.
The aa column adds up to $p^2q^2 + 2pq^3 + q^4$, or $q^2 (p^2 + 2pq + q^2)$, or q^2.

This mathematical formulation of the theoretical relationships between allelic genes is based on certain assumptions about the population. In order for the frequencies of each allele to remain the same, these assumptions must be true:

1. *No mutation*—That is, no genes are changing through spontaneous mutation.
2. *No natural selection*—There is no difference in survival value of the genotypes.
3. *No genetic drift*—The population is of adequate size to insure that no genes are lost through chance owing to small sample size.
4. *No migration*—No new genes are brought in through gene admixture, which would upset the population composition.
5. *Random mating*—All gene combinations are equally likely (any restriction on mating imposed by family lineage systems or social boundaries will reduce the random reshuffling of genetic material every generation).
6. *Infinite size*—Such a mathematical formulation as the Hardy-Weinberg equilibrium assumes that the sample is infinite.

Of course, all of these conditions do not always hold, especially in the case of human populations. The formula and the conditions for the existence define an ideal situation that is not encountered in the natural world. What good, then, is the Hardy-Weinberg formula? It serves as a reference point against which genetic change can be measured as it takes place between the generations. In a sense it is comparable to the gas laws in physics, which describe the behavior of a perfect gas under standard conditions of pressure and temperature. Here, also, the formula only approximates the actual situation.

This chapter has provided an overview of the biological basis of human inheritance and variability. These basic concepts will be developed throughout the balance of the book and appropriate examples given. The examples offer evidence that man is subject to basic biological laws. Though his behavior may alter the direct effect of the forces acting on a species, his total gene combinations are still related to certain environmental variables that exert selective forces. The appreciation of the importance of these forces will enable us to trace man's evolution and to understand his biological diversity.

RECOMMENDED READINGS AND
LITERATURE CITED

CAVALLI-SFORZA, L. L. and W. F. BODMER. 1971. *The Genetics of Human Populations.* San Francisco: W. H. Freeman and Co.

DOBZHANSKY, T. 1970. *Genetics and the Evolutionary Process.* New York: Columbia University Press.

JOHNSTON, FRANCIS E. 1973. *Micro-Evolution of Human Populations.* Englewood Cliffs, N.J.: Prentice-Hall, Inc.

McKUSICK, VICTOR A. 1969. *Human Genetics.* Englewood Cliffs, N.J.: Prentice-Hall, Inc.

MAYR, ERNST. 1963. *Animal Species and Evolution.* Cambridge, Mass.: The Belknap Press of Harvard University.

NEEL, JAMES V., F. M. SALZANO, P. C. JUNQUEIRA, F. KEITER, and D. MAYBERRY LEWIS. 1964. "Studies on the Xavante Indians of the Brazilian Mato Grosso," *Am. J. Human Genetics,* 16(1): 52–140.

chapter three

Man's
Biology

Human biological variability, as described earlier, is determined by interaction between the environment and genetic systems. The traits that we study and use in comparisons of interpopulation variability can be divided into two groups: polygenic and monogenic. The polygenic traits are apparently more complex, owing to interaction of several genes, and are more subject to environmental influences. The resultant phenotype is continuously variable over a broad range, particularly in the case of such phenotypes as skin color or body form.

Single-gene traits are considerably easier to deal with in terms of their mode of inheritance, and many of these phenotypes are little influenced by the environment. Such traits include the several blood-group systems, abnormal hemoglobins, and serum proteins. This list is continuously growing as new polymorphisms are identified, many of them part of enzyme systems or proteins in the blood serum. These traits are discontinuous; the trait is either present or absent. Single-gene traits provide significant information about polymorphism of man's genetic system; we shall examine them in the second section of this chapter.

THE HUMAN FORM
AND ITS RANGE OF VARIABILITY

> I have measured crania and heads, skeletons and bodies, for many a year. If I have learned one thing it is this: similarity is not identity and "looks alike" does not point to common origin. . . . Dixon took a few cranial measurements and indices and found "Australoids" all over the world, Dart did much the same and found "Nordics" liberally sprinkled throughout Africa, and Hooton found "Mediterranean" and "Negroids" in prehistoric Pecos. A given cranial length and breadth and their ratio in two dolichocranic peoples need not bespeak a genetic (heritability related) similarity. (Krogman, 1971: 442)

The different sizes, shapes and colors of the world's peoples are often described as representative of certain distinct groups, each possessing special typical features. Seldom, however, do we appreciate that the range of man's diversity extends in gradual degrees throughout the species. Another problem is that we are so familiar with *H. sapiens* that we take many of our species' traits for granted. Because of this difficulty, and because we tend to see in our species a model or an ideal type, it is best to review some of the traits man shares with the other primates, and also to consider how populations are both similar and different, and how they vary from one region of the world to the next.

Man, as a primate, has a large number of anatomical features that are rather general and are shared by many other species of this group. These characteristics consist mainly of anatomical modifications which seem to have been related to an arboreal adaptation in the past:

1. The limbs have special features such as a five-digit grasping appendage with an opposable thumb or great toe. The ends of these digits have a flattened nail instead of a claw, and the skin has a special friction surface (a dermal ridge that leaves fingerprints).
2. The thoracic or chest region of the body is especially modified to serve as an anchorage for mobile forelimbs or arms, having a well-developed clavicle and a chest flattened in the dorsal-ventral direction.
3. The head of the primate has many unique features also, such as the forwardly directed orbits of the eye, which are completely surrounded with a ring of bone. This enables the primate to have binocular vision and, thus, depth perception, necessary for an arboreal creature. The snout region is much reduced in comparison to other mammals, and the cranial portion is expanded to enclose a proportionally larger brain.

Each species of primate possesses these characteristics to a certain degree, together with certain of its own specialized features. The human species shares with the pongids (great apes) a number of similarities; there is no bone in man, for example, that is not present in the apes. In fact, man and the apes are placed taxonomically in the same group—superfamily Hominoidea. In subsequent sections, when head and body proportions are considered, one can readily see that many of the anatomical distinctions of man are a matter of degree rather than kind when compared to the pongids.

However, a few traits do set man apart, such as the relatively hairless body, the large brain-body ratio, and bipedal locomotion. The large cranial size and the reduced face size are unique, so that even an amateur could hardly confuse a modern human skull with that of a great ape. The pelvic girdle and the human foot, adapted for bipedal locomotion, also are quite distinctively human. Both structures demonstrate that through evolutionary processes the Hominid form has adapted to a specialized form of behavior which anthropologists call *culture*—the learned behavioral pattern that man uses to manipulate the environment in order to survive. Through this environmental-behavior interaction the selective forces acting on man are altered and, as we shall see, change the gene-pool composition from generation to generation.

Through environmental alteration Hominid evolution has proceeded for several million years. Man's brain case has expanded and his face and teeth have diminished. The bones of the pelvic girdle began to change very early during this period, making it possible for man to walk erect as a normal means of locomotion. Erect walking may have provided the anatomical basis for a mode of behavior which was part of a shift in the feeding and foraging activities of man's immediate ancestors. This in turn established a system of interaction between prehistoric man's behavior and his anatomy (Figure 3-1).

Body Size

Man's form varies over a wide range of sizes and shapes, and there is considerable difference among human populations living today. From pygmoid peoples to tall slender Nilotics of East Africa, and from Eskimos to Southern Europeans, we find that the ratio between stature and body weight varies in a way that may reflect environmental conditions.

The height of normal adults in our species ranges from around four feet to well over six feet. These limits are exceeded occasionally but seem to represent a norm for modern stature. It should be noted that females are generally 5 to 10 percent smaller than males. The tendency today in many populations is towards an increase in stature, owing partly to

FIGURE 3-1

Schematic of Bio-Cultural Interaction

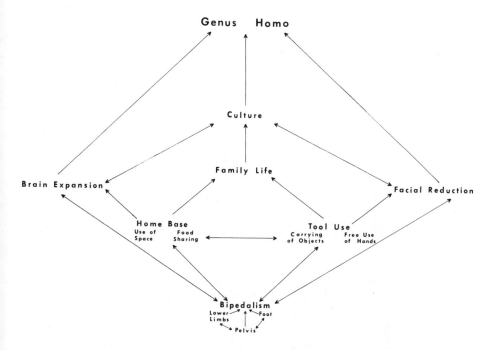

improved diet (especially increased protein during the early part of growth) and to a reduction of infectious diseases in early childhood. A tendency to increase in height will not continue indefinitely, even with an increased improvement in living standards. Some populations have, in fact, reached their genetic potential for maximum stature and no further increase is expected.

This variation of man's stature is distributed among the world's peoples in some very interesting ways. Though there appears to be a tendency toward taller people far from the equator (as in Northwestern Europe) and toward shorter people nearer the equator, numerous exceptions exist. There are many examples of tall people living close to very short or even pygmoid groups. For instance, the Mbuti pygmies of the Ituri Forest in the Congo are just a short distance from a group who are considered the tallest people in the world, the Watusi. Every racial or ethnic group seems to have its tall and short peoples, and stature covers such a broad range that general statements are precluded.

Body weight also varies over a wide range but does not necessarily correlate with stature: some tall people are light in weight compared to much shorter people. Man's adult weight ranges from about seventy pounds to over two hundred. Generally, body size is distributed in the world's populations in a way that seems to correlate with mean annual temperatures; the heavier people tend to be located in the colder climates. Though quantity of diet influences body weight, the effects of climate are often evident, as in the case of large groups of U.S. Army recruits from the colder states who were consistently heavier than those from the more southern states.

There seems to be little racial variation in body weight or in response to a surplus dietary intake. However, there are some striking examples of racial differences in weight distribution, as in the case of *steatopygia* in Bushman women, who develop enormous buttocks when they are well fed. This may allow storage of excess body energy without reducing the body's ability to dissipate metabolic heat. Most peoples of the world store excess dietary calories as a layer of fat below the skin surface; the fat layer evenly distributed over most of the body acts as insulation and would reduce loss of body heat through radiation, a decided disadvantage in the heat of the Kalahari Desert where the Bushmen live.

A number of interesting groups of people in the world are very small; these people are commonly called pygmies or Negrillos in Africa or Negritos in South East Asia. A number of populations in these regions look so similar that early travelers believed they were all members of the same racial group.

In Africa approximately 150,000 Pygmies live today in small groups scattered throughout the tropical rainforest area of Central Africa, from near Lake Tanganyika in East Africa to French Equatorial Africa and the Cameroon in the west. Modern Pygmies are believed to be remnants of an ancient group of tropical forest dwellers who lived from Liberia to Rwanda. These populations have been progressively reduced and thinly scattered over the area as agriculturalists began to occupy portions of the tropical rainforest approximately two thousand years ago. The Pygmies have been pushed farther and farther into the more remote, agriculturally less desirable regions until today the largest numbers of Pygmies in Africa are concentrated in Central Africa around the basin areas of the tributaries of the Congo River. The best known of these groups, such as the Efe, Batwa, and Bakanga, live in the regions to the East of Kisangani (Stanleyville) in Zaire. However, a few groups, such as the Babinza, live in the western region of Central Africa, and these western groups are less numerous and more scattered.

Groups called Negritos, sometimes referred to as Oceania Pygmies, live dispersed in many remote areas throughout Southeast Asia. They are found in the jungles of the Malayan Peninsula and on the island of Sumatra; these are the Semang and the Senoi (Sakal), who are slightly taller with a mean stature of 152 cm (five feet). Off the west coast of the Malayan Peninsula are the Andaman Islands, inhabited by three distinct groups of Negritos: the Minicopies, the Onge, and the Garawa. They all are similar in features and a bit shorter than the Semang, 149 cm (four feet ten inches). The Onge are quite fat, and the women develop large fleshy buttocks similar to the steatopygia of the Bushman females. On the Philippine Islands of Mindanao, Palawan, and the northern part of Luzon are a few remnants of pygmoid populations. Among the best known are the Aetas, whose mean stature has been given as 147 cm (four feet nine inches). The final Negrito groups are found in the remotest parts of the mountains of western New Guinea; the Tapiro tribe are an example with a mean stature of 144 cm (four feet seven inches).

The general characteristics of the Negritos, besides small stature, are very dark skin color, woolly hair, scant body and facial hairs, broad nose, and slight to moderately developed brow ridges. All groups do not share equally in these features, and there is a considerable variation between certain populations. In the case of skin color, some Negritos as in the Philippine populations are lighter brown or even yellowish, while the Andaman Islanders have very dark brown to black skin. Facial features also differ considerably, from smooth rounded foreheads to heavy brows (usually in New Guinea groups) that match well the faces of many Australian Aborigines.

The Pygmy problem is the question: are the two divisions, African and Southeast Asian, related in any way? Do they, as once supposed, share close common ancestry, or are they members of a pygmoid race? Casual visual comparisons suggest they are descendants from the same ancestor because of their comparable size, skin color, and hair form. Often Pygmies and Negritos have been classified as a single race, and certain anthropologists have even plotted elaborate migration routes to get the ancestors of Southeast Asian Negritos from an African homeland to their present distribution. But other studies of Pygmies and Negritos have pointed out that they are two independent types with only short stature in common (see Boyd, 1963).

Although the Pygmies-Negritos are indeed the smallest known humans, numerous other groups have representative populations that are relatively short. Rather than being restricted to a particular race, short stature occurs in several divisions of mankind. If the Pygmy is not considered separately but as a part of the total species and if he is compared to other populations, then the extent of his uniqueness decreases. In fact dwarf peoples, in general, may be no more than local inbred populations (see Abbie, 1967), Figure 3-2 gives statures for several populations of our species, and though the Pygmy is at the low end of the range, several groups have comparably short stature. Though these groups

FIGURE 3-2
Diagram of Stature Variation between Populations

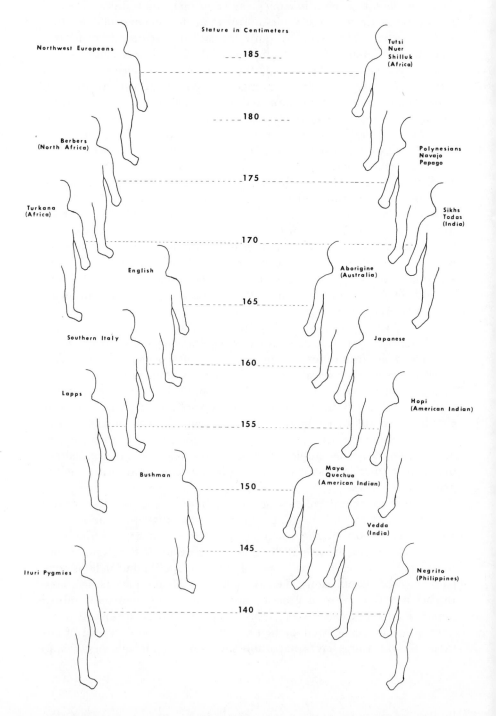

Stature in Centimeters

Northwest Europeans

Tutsi
Nuer
Shilluk
(Africa)

185

180

Berbers
(North Africa)

Polynesians
Navajo
Papago

175

Turkana
(Africa)

Sikhs
Todas
(India)

170

English

Aborigine
(Australia)

165

Southern Italy

Japanese

160

Lapps

Hopi
(American Indian)

155

Bushman

Maya
Quechua
(American Indian)

150

Vedda
(India)

145

Ituri Pygmies

Negrito
(Philippines)

140

are taller, the range of variation of adjacent populations on the chart shows considerable overlap. It is necessary to consider this factor of variability in biological populations if human variation is to be understood in its relationship to the selective forces in the environment.

Many populations show a tendency towards a particular body form. Like stature, however, this characteristic varies too much to be used as a racial criterion. A relatively simple way of determining body proportion is to compare a person's standing height with his sitting height. The *cormic index* [1] or ratio between the two measurements indicates proportion of stature due to the legs or the trunk. In populations with relatively short torsos and long legs, as in the Australian Aborigines and many Africans, the cormic index is less than 50 (a ratio of 50 would indicate the legs and trunk plus head were approximately the same length). The large stature of the Nilotic groups in East Africa north of Lake Victoria (Dinka, Shilluk, Nuer) is due largely to their very long legs, while most descriptions of the Pygmies note their elongated trunks with short legs and long arms. Many Chinese populations as well as groups of American Indians and Eskimos have cormic indices as high as 54 percent, which indicates rather long trunks and short legs. These proportions probably have adaptive significance and may be related to climatic factors.

The ratio between height and weight of the individual may be even more significant than limb ratios or trunk limb proportions (see Table 3-1). Generally speaking, in colder climates people are much heavier for their height than people in hotter countries. Though dietary quantity and quality affect bodily proportions, there is a close correlation with mean annual temperature. All racial groups consist of some populations who have high stature-weight ratios (which indicates a tall thin person) as well as groups with low ratios (short and heavy). In the groups from the warmer regions, particularly the Bushmen of the Kalahari Desert and the Australian Aborigines, there is a tendency to have a slender build; populations in the temperate or arctic regions are heavier for their stature for example, Eskimos, North Chinese, and Icelanders.

These examples of body variability under different conditions of diet and climate demonstrate the great plasticity of *H. sapiens*. This characteristic has been documented by many studies of migrant populations, most recently in a study of stature increase among second-generation Italian Americans in the Boston area (Damon, 1965). Stature increased from the oldest to the youngest age groups sampled, which were divided into decades from 20–29 to 50–59. This suggests that as economic standards and hence living conditions improve, the population stature increases.

---

[1] Sitting height divided by standing height.

TABLE 3-1

Body Size and Stature-Weight Ratio [1]

Population (Males)	Stature (Centimeters)	Weight (Kilograms)	Ratio
Kazakh (Turkestan)	163.1	69.7	2.34
Finland	171.0	70.0	2.44
Iceland	173.6	68.1	2.55
Eskimo	161.2	62.9	2.56
England	166.3	64.5	2.58
Sicily	169.1	65.0	2.60
Venezuela	164.2	62.4	2.61
Ecuador	157.7	57.5	2.73
North China	168.0	61.0	2.75
Scotland	170.4	61.8	2.76
Yambasa (Africa)	169.0	62.0	2.78
Berbers	169.8	59.5	2.85
Korea	161.1	55.5	2.90
Mahratta (India)	163.8	55.7	2.94
Central China	163.0	54.7	2.98
Thailand	161.0	53.2	3.03
Japan	160.9	53.0	3.04
Sundanese	159.8	51.9	3.08
Annamites	158.7	51.3	3.09
Batutsi (Africa)	176.0	57.0	3.09
Kikuyu	164.5	51.9	3.17
Hong Kong	166.2	52.2	3.18
Vietnam	157.6	49.1	3.21
Burma	161.5	49.9	3.24
India	163.0	48.2	3.38
Efe	143.8	39.8	3.61
Pygmies	142.2	39.9	3.56
Bushmen	155.8	40.4	3.86

[1] Based on Dobzhensky, 1962, and Frisch and Revelle, 1969.

Head Size and Shape

The shape and size of the head have been under intense study by many generations of anthropologists, and numerous descriptive measurements have been devised. The human head has been of special interest because of the wealth of well-preserved skulls from prehistoric times. Representative skulls from ancient extinct populations often show characteristics that apparently set them apart and have been used to establish relationships between past and present populations.

Among the many skull features examined, the one most frequently used in the past for establishing racial groups has been the cephalic index, as noted earlier (see page 11). This index, the ratio of the breadth to the length of the skull, provides an approximation of the skull's shape as viewed from the top. The skull of our species varies from long and narrow to short and broad—a variation of cephalic index from 70 (breadth =70 percent of length) to about 90.

The index has to be discounted as a racial criterion, because it is not a simple character depending on one gene but rather is determined by a multiple gene complex; also it is subject to strong environmental influences. However, certain populations tend to be more broad-headed than others, and the index is distributed around the world in a way which led earlier students to believe that racial groupings could be described on this basis. For example, on the average, Africans tend to have the narrowest heads except for Australian Aborigines, while Andean Indians and Central Europeans have the broadest (see Table 3-2). A recent study

TABLE 3-2

Cephalic Indexes [1]

Group	Mean Index
Central Bantu	74.1
South Africa (Bushmen, Hottentots)	75.1
Vedda	75.6
Ituri Pygmies	76.5
New Guinea and Melanesia	77.7
Eskimo	78.0
Madagascar and Indian Ocean	78.7
Sioux (central U.S.A.)	79.6
Iran, Armenia, Assyria	80.2
Japanese	80.8
Norwegians	81.0
E. Chinese	81.7
Germans	82.5
Negritos (Philippines)	82.7
Hawaiians	84.0
Norwegian Lapps	85.0

[1] Based on Weiner, et al., 1964, and Kelso, 1972, and others.

by Beals (1972) suggests a correlation between head shape and temperature: populations in colder climates have rounder heads.

On the basis of this measure alone, as can be seen from the chart (which shows similar indices for such disparate groups as Andeans and Central Europeans, Norwegians and Otomis), it is impossible to use only cephalic index as a measure of race. However, there is a component of inheritance in head shape, as demonstrated by Osborne and De George (1959), who compared monozygotic with dizygotic twins. There also appears to be a positive correlation between stature and skull length: taller individuals have longer heads. Because of these factors, plus the pattern of distribution of cranial shape, cephalic index remains an element of interest in the study of bodily proportions, and it should be considered as a part of the overall growth and development pattern.

Cranial Capacity and Brain Size

More nonsense has, perhaps, been written about the size of the human brain and its relationship to intelligence than about any other aspect of man. This is probably because the size of the brain case or cranial vault increases throughout the fossil record of man's evolution (Table 3-3). The estimated volume of the cranial vault has increased

TABLE 3-3
Range of Cranial Capacity in Some
Fossil and Modern Men, Including Two Pongids [1]

	Range of Cranial Capacities
Chimpanzee	275–500 cm^3
Gorilla	340–752
Australopithecine	450–700 (approx.)
Homo erectus	775–1200
(Pithecanthropus,	
Sinanthropus)	
Neanderthal	1100–1640
Homo sapiens	1000–1700

[1] Based on Schultz, 1926, Montagu, 1960, and Tobias, 1971.

from a low of 450 cubic centimeters in one of the earliest hominids—the Australopithecines—to the highest in modern man. But the modern range of brain space was achieved quite early in human evolution, approximately 100,000 years ago, during the Neanderthal phase. In fact, the estimated mean size of the Neanderthal (1450 cc) is higher than the mean for modern man (1345 cc).

That the brain space and hence the brain has increased in size during the last two million years of evolution is extremely important in studies of human paleontology, and comparison of cranial capacities of the different fossils can be useful. In modern populations (Table 3-4) there is such a wide range in variation that the lower end of the range is well below the capacity for certain fossil hominids, yet there is no evidence that these individuals are any less intelligent than persons with larger cranial vaults. It is unlikely that the differences in modern population brain size have any relevance to variation in mental ability— a factor that renders comparisons of cranial capacity between modern groups a futile and meaningless exercise. As Von Bonin (1963), a foremost neuroanatomist, once stated, the correlation between brain size

TABLE 3-4

Mean Cranial Capacity [1]

Group	Capacity in Cubic Centimeters
Australian Aborigines	1256
New Guinea	1280
Veddas	1285
African Negroes	1346
English	1386
Czechs	1438
South American Indians	1442
Western Eskimo	1473
English	1480
Koreans	1490
Mongols	1573

[1] Based on Montagu, 1960, and others.

and mental capacity is insignificant in modern man. A good example can be seen in the case of females who have, on the average, 10 percent smaller cranial capacities than males; no one has dared suggest that this indicates lower mental capacity. Also, many famous men in history have, upon their deaths, had their brain weighed and measured, and the ranges encompassed the total range for *H. sapiens,* from Anatole France (cranial capacity of approximately 1100 cc) to Oliver Cromwell and Lord Byron (cranial capacity of approximately 2200 cc). Nevertheless, there are authors, even today, who insist on recording and emphasizing racial differences in cranial capacity as if it were a meaningful indicator.[2] Table 3-4 lists some select groups, but before the reader draws any conclusions it should be pointed out that variation of plus or minus 400 cc about the mean is seen in most European populations. These individuals with larger or smaller cranial capacities are normally functioning and intellectually competent individuals; in fact, there are many persons with 700 to 800 cubic centimeters.

The major changes during the evolution of man's brain have been qualitative rather than merely a gross alteration in size.[3] In addition, it is not so much a matter of gross size as it is a ratio of brain to body size. Man's brain weighs approximately 2 percent of his total body weight, or a ratio of one to forty-five, while the gorilla brain/body ratio is one to four hundred. However, even though man stands near the top of the list of primates in brain/body weight ratios, his is not the largest (see Table 3-5). The marmoset (the smallest platyrhine monkey of South America)

[2] For a discussion of brain size see Phillip W. Tobias, "Brain Size, Grey Matter and Race—Fact or Fiction," *Am. J. Phys. Anthrop.,* 32(1): 3–26, 1970.

[3] See Ralph L. Holloway, "Cranial Capacity and Neuron Number," *Am. J. Phys. Anthrop.,* 25: 305–314, 1966.

TABLE 3-5

Brain/Body Ratios

Species	Body Weight	Brain/Body
Man	61.5 Kg	1:47
Chimp	56.7	1:129
Gorilla	250	1:420
Night Monkey	9	1:84
Capuchin	3.1	1:43
Galago	0.2	1:40
Deer	65	1:310
Rat	0.2	1:122

has a ratio of one to nineteen, and the squirrel monkey of South America a ratio of one to twelve. However, no one would argue that these primate brains were qualitatively comparable to man's, for as Holloway (1966: 108) states: "One c.c. of chimpanzee cortex is not equivalent to one c.c. of human cortex, nor is it likely that any equivalent measure can be found."

Racial variations in the brain weight of man often are used to support a contention that there are severe differences in the innate mental capacities of certain populations.[4] These variations in brain weight may prove to be no more significant than cranial capacity or cephalic index in terms of correlations with mental capacities, however measured. This is because of several variables that effect brain weight but are seldom mentioned—especially the factor of growth and brain development.

During the first five years of life the individual's brain grows at an accelerated rate to achieve 90 percent of its adult weight—50 percent of the adult weight during the first six months of life. If the individual is malnourished during this period, a significant reduction in weight will result, sometimes up to 20 percent. Where the body generally will recover from malnutrition with improved diet and will actually "catch up" to achieve its adult potential (as in body stature), the brain will probably not recover and its weight loss is permanent. Another factor affecting brain weight is the aging process, which causes a loss of about 10 percent of the total brain weight. Any comparison between brain weights must take into account the age of the specimen and the nutritional level during the critical growth period of early childhood.

In the numerous statements that have been made on racial intelligence, no consideration has been given to the positive correlation between body height and brain weight. As described earlier, man's stature varies over a wide range; and, since brain weight is correlated with stature, it

4 See such authors as Weyl and Possony, 1963: 53–56, and Putnam, 1967: 48–53.

would make little sense, and reveal nothing about brain quality, to compare, for example, brains of Northern Europeans with brains of Bushmen, Pygmies, or any other group unless brain weights were corrected for body-height differences.

These and other factors affecting brain weight, in addition to the many problems of technique involved in actually obtaining brain weights, make any interpopulation comparison extremely difficult. Finally, it appears that at this stage of our knowledge about brain size, weight, and quality, little can be said about the innate intelligence in man from a study of the gross dimensions of brain, and any so-called comparative studies of supposed racial differences are doomed to failure.

Face Form

The human face is highly variable in its shape and size, and distinctly individual forms occur. We can easily recognize our friends by their facial appearance, and we automatically group people according to their expressions or dimensions and proportions of the face. But any scheme devised to describe facial characteristics of certain populations is just a rough approximation which will include only a small portion of the individuals in the group. One worker went so far as to divide faces into ten different categories or types, from the elliptical to oval, including such terms as rectangular and pentagonal. But even with many gradations between these categories it was still impossible to apply them to all members of a population.

Evolutionarily man's face has changed a great deal from the heavy prognathic structure, possessed by our fossil ancestors, to the flattened structure in modern man that is rather small in contrast to the large human head. This change has come about through evolutionary processes, as our ancestors relied less on their jaws and teeth for procuring and manipulating food, which, in turn, reduced natural selection for large facial bones. The structures of the face, whose major function is to support the chewing apparatus, therefore diminished in size.[5] These structures are primarily the brow ridges (the ridge of bone over the eyes), the cheek bones (or zygomatic arches), and of course the upper and lower arches of bone that support the teeth. With a reduction in these elements the human face began to take on a new look and the proportions altered drastically. However, all of the world's populations did not undergo exactly the same pattern of change, nor were their faces altered at the same rate. Many of the facial features maintained rather large sizes in some populations, such as the Eskimo and Australian Aborigines.

[5] For a discussion of these functions see Brace and Mahler, 1971, and Brace, 1963.

One rather distinctive facial characteristic clearly involved in the evolutionary process is prognathism, the forward protrusion of dental arches. A comparison of modern man with recent or ancient and fossil Neanderthals illustrates the reduction in the lower face of modern man (Figure 3-3). Many modern populations today have prognathic profiles, yet this does not indicate a close affinity with fossil ancestors; rather, it is the result of the presence of large teeth. Since the major purpose of the bony structures in this part of the face is the support of the dentition, the bone arches of the maxilla and mandible are correspondingly large.

Man's teeth [6] are often ignored when human variability is considered, despite their importance as evidence in evolution and adaptation to environmental conditions. Teeth served man well as cutting, grinding, and shearing implements in past times, as the well-worn dental remains of prehistoric man demonstrate (see Brace, 1962, also Molnar, 1971). In

FIGURE 3-3

Alveolar Prognathism

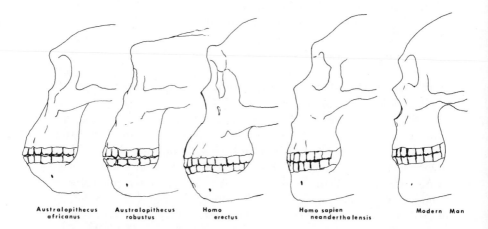

| Australopithecus africanus | Australopithecus robustus | Homo erectus | Homo sapien neanderthalensis | Modern Man |

[6] The Old World primates and man possess four basic types of permanent teeth:

(a) The front teeth or incisors are broad and spatulate-shaped, especially adapted at cutting and shearing.

(b) The canines or "eye teeth" at the corners of the arches are sturdy, long-rooted teeth, which in man function much like the incisors.

(c) The premolars, between the canines and molars, are sturdy structures frequently used to bite off hard objects that prove to be difficult for the incisors. They also aid in the grinding and chopping of the food.

(d) The molars, the final three teeth in each side of the dental arches, are used for grinding. Their multicusped crowns increase the efficiency of the grinding operation.

fact, fossil man's survival as well as most recent human populations depended a great deal on a sturdy dentition and a heavy, well-formed skeleton. However, with the rise of technological efficiency in dealing with the raw materials necessary to sustain life, there was less reliance on the dental arches as implements; so in modern times our teeth often are looked upon as annoying items in our anatomy which frequently require dental treatment.

Because of their importance in the past, man's teeth have characteristics which increased the dentition's utilty as chewing implements. Throughout man's evolution these characteristics varied from population to population so that, today, the racial groups of the world show considerable diversity in these dental features due to the differences in selective forces that have been operating on each group. Tooth size shows great variation, especially the diameter of the molar crown. From the large crowns of the Australopithecine molars (approximately 15 mm diameter in the cheek-to-tongue direction) to the small sizes seen in many European populations (11.5 mm diameter of the first molar) the dentition of man and his ancestors have steadily reduced in size. This reduction has not been equal in all of the world's peoples, and some today, such as the Australian Aborigines, still possess large teeth (see Table 3-6).

Another dental feature that occurs in certain populations more frequently then others is *shovel-shaped* incisors. This term describes an incisor tooth which has thickened margins on the lingual surface (tongue side of the tooth). These raised surfaces provide structural reinforcement that prevents or reduces the possibility of breakage. In the Mongoloid groups most individuals have these types of incisors, and children in these groups suffer far less from breakage of the upper central incisors than children in European populations.

Several other features of the dentition show a great deal of variability and, in some cases, have been grouped according to race. More often, though, there is only a variability in the frequency of the occurrence of the particular trait, with all the major groups of mankind possessing it to some degree. The molar cusps are an example, since their number and arrangement on the molar crown has often been incorrectly used to identify racial affinity. Some groups frequently do tend to have one or another pattern; for example, there are five cusps on the lower first molar of the Australian Aborigine, whereas the first molars of many Europeans tend to be reduced in size and have only four cusps. However, a good many individual Aborigines differ from this "typical" pattern, often having a sixth cusp. So it is with other "racial" characteristics of the teeth: though a group may have a higher frequency of one or more dental traits, they are seldom unique possessors and other segments of

TABLE 3-6

Dimensions of Lower First Molar of Fossil and Modern Men

(After M. Wolpoff, 1971)

	Length (M-D)		Breadth (B-L)	
	Mean	*Range*	*Mean*	*Range*
H. Africanus	13.87	11.60–16.50	13.04	11.30–15.00
H. Robustus	14.57	11.80–16.40	13.77	11.50–15.50
H. Erectus	12.74	9.90–14.70	12.02	10.10–13.70
H. Neanderthal	11.69	8.00–14.00	11.13	9.00–12.70
H. Sapiens	11.55	9.00–14.10	10.99	8.30–13.00
Australopithecines	14.34	11.60–16.50	13.53	11.30–15.50
Neanderthal	11.41	8.00–14.00	10.97	9.00–12.70
Mt. Carmel	11.56	10.50–13.00	11.18	10.50–11.50
Austr. Aborigine	12.30	11.00–14.00	11.90	10.00–13.50
Pecos Pueblo	11.96	10.78–13.01	10.74	9.46–11.92
American Whites (2)	11.90	10.10–13.20	10.60	9.60–11.40
American Negroes	11.90	10.60–13.40	10.80	9.80–11.90
E. Greenland Eskimo	11.81	10.60–12.60	11.32	10.10–12.50
Sub Saharan (Africa)	11.77	9.50–14.10	11.16	8.80–13.00
New Britain	11.75	10.00–13.60	11.36	10.10–12.60
American Indian	11.68	10.00–13.30	11.28	10.00–12.45
Gillmanuk (Indon.)	11.60	10.00–13.40	11.00	9.60–12.20
Aleuts	11.45	10.10–12.80	10.50	9.20–11.30
Caucasoid	11.21	9.80–13.00	10.74	9.20–12.70
American Whites (1)	10.95	9.40–12.70		
Bushmen	10.90	10.00–12.00	10.20	9.00–11.30
Lapps	10.80	9.20–12.80	10.22	8.30–12.20

mankind have the same traits (as in the case of shovel-shaped incisors, Table 3-7). To sum up, the range of variability of the dentition of modern

TABLE 3-7

Shovel-Shape in Upper Median Incisors [1]

Population	*Percent Male*	*Percent Female*
Chinese	66–89	82–94
Japanese	78	–
Mongolian	62–91	91
Eskimo	84	84
Pima Indians	96	99
Pueblo Indians	86–89	86–89
Aleut	96	–
American Negro	12	11
American White	9	8

[1] Based on Carbonell, 1963, and Comas, 1960.

man is so great that several characteristic features must be taken into account before racial or population affinity is described.

Nose Form

The shape of the human face is primarily organized around two major structures: the chewing apparatus and the nose. The nose dominates the midfacial region of man, the height of the nasal opening being about 60 percent of facial height. The nose varies a great deal in size and shape, and no one shape or form is possessed typically by any single race.

Nasal index (a ratio of the length to the width of the nose) is the most frequent way of describing shape. An index of 104 would describe a nose slightly wider at the nostrils than it is long; it is found among the Pygmies of the Ituri Forest area in Central Africa and a few Australian Aborigines. Narrower noses, represented by low indices (85 and below), are found among many groups throughout the world, in many American Indians, North Africans, many Europeans, and Eskimos. A narrow or a broad nose form is not confined to any particular race; for example, long narrow noses are found among the Negro peoples occupying the highlands of East Africa, are in contrast to the wide noses of the tropical dweller in the Congo Basin.

Nose form is a function largely of climatic factors, such as temperature and moisture content of the air, rather then a simple result of racial affinities. The nose serves to moisten the inspired air, so in the drier regions of the world people have noses which possess the greatest surface area of mucous membrane, a condition achieved by the longer, more narrow nose form; so among desert and mountain peoples the narrow nose is predominant.[7] Even in the cold and drier climates the Eskimos have a narrow nasal aperture, which provides an efficient mechanism for warming as well as moistening the inspired air. It is a simple matter of fact that a high narrow nasal opening can warm and moisten air more efficiently than a short broad one, and in climates where the moisture content of the air is very low, selective forces act on this particular nose form, whether the dryness is due to intense heat or intense cold (Table 3-8).

Since face form is due to the interaction of the growth processes of several facial bones, any single feature is the result of interacting forces. This is especially true of nose form, whose width is correlated with climate, as noted above, but also with the size and proportion of the

---

[7] For a thorough discussion see M. Wolpoff, "Climatic Influence on the Skeletal Nasal Aperture," *Am. J. Phys. Anthrop.* 29(3): 405–424, 1968.

TABLE 3-8
Mean Nasal Indexes of Select Populations

Population	Mean Nasal Index
South African Bushmen	103.9
Mbuti Pygmies	103.8
Aborigines (Australia)	99.6
Northern Bantu	95.5
Central Bantu	93.8
Vedda (India)	85.5
American Indian (Plains)	72.0
Eskimo	68.5
European	66.0
Iran	63.7

upper dental arch. As the palate gets wider, the nasal aperture becomes broader. The case of the Australian Aborigines is a good example; though they live in a very dry area of the world, their noses are extremely broad, and this dimension is related to the chewing processes exerted on the palate during growth in childhood, which stimulates the palate to develop. Also, prognathism tends to be associated with a short broad nose, and a significant correlation has been found between the length of the skull base and nasal width.

These factors of climatic influence and structural interrelationships suggest that human face form is extremely complex, numerous variables being involved in growth and development. Conclusions should not be drawn about relationships between two populations on the basis of a similarity in structure, because face form (like the small stature in Pygmies and Negritos discussed above) develops according to local factors of natural selection. It is not necessary to postulate migrations and inter-mixtures to explain similarities between populations, as once was done for the Nilotic face form found in groups like the Nuer, Shilluk, and others in East Africa. At one time their long straight noses were believed to be due to contact and interbreeding with Caucasoid groups from Western Asia. Subsequent genetic studies have not borne this theory out. No doubt, over a period of thousands of years, contact with Western Asian populations had taken place and some interbreeding had resulted, but people with the Nilotic face are the result of local selective forces acting on the population; it is not merely a matter of interbreeding between races.

The Human Skin

The human body is clothed in a protective layer of skin consisting of two major layers, the dermis and epidermis. The innermost or *dermal* layer contains the blood vessels, nerves, hair follicles, and gland cells (sweat, sabaecous, and apocrine). This layer is covered by a protective sheath of *epidermis,* which protects it from the outside environment, especially solar radiation. Epidermis is a tissue of four layers which act together to provide the basic protection of the body as well as to synthesize a vital hormone-vitamin (calciferol or vitamin D_3).

The lowest layer or *stratum germinativum* contains long columnar cells which make contact with the deeper layer or dermis; within this layer also are specialized cells, the *melanocytes,* which synthesize the brown-black pigment granules, melanin. These granules are found scattered throughout the upper layers of the epidermis. The next layer is the *stratum granulosum,* where cells which synthesize the protein keratin are found. *Keratin* is a major constituent of nails, hair, and the outer flaky layer of skin. The final layers are the *stratum lucidum* and *corneum,* which are composed of fused cells. This outermost region of the skin varies considerably in thickness from one region of the body to the next, the more protected layers being thinner, while areas like the palms of the hands and the soles of the feet are relatively thick.

The skin, in addition to its protective role, has many varied functions. It is a storehouse for chlorides; a heat-regulatory organ, with the erectopapillae fibers able to contract the skin and reduce heat loss (the cause of goose bumps); a tactile organ; and a factory producing a pigment (melanin) and vitamin D. Because of our concern with human racial differences, and since skin color has been the major sorting criteria, the importance of melanin will be considered at length.

The color of *Homo sapiens'* skin, an easily perceived trait, has been used for many centuries as a criterion to divide man into racial groups. Even the terms Black, Brown, White, and Yellow are widely applied and accepted as devices for easily distinguishing between groups of our species. The belief that man comes in a few primary shades is well ingrained in our culture, as is the belief that similarity of color indicates common ancestry. However, the facts are quite different, and perhaps in no other character is man so diverse as in his skin coloration. We come in all varieties, from the very pale Lapplanders to the dark brown inhabitants of the tropical rainforest of Central Africa, such as the Pygmies or their neighbors, the Bantu. Even within the same population there is a significant difference in pigmentation between males and females.[8] This

[8] See F. S. Hulse, "Selection for Skin Color Among the Japanese," *Am. J. Phys. Anthrop.,* 27: 143–154, 1967.

variation is due to several factors such as the blood in the innermost layer of the skin (dermis), which gives lighter-skinned people their pinkish hue, and keratin, which is present in outer layers and has a yellowish tinge. However, the light or darkness of the human skin depends mainly on the amount of melanin present. *Melanin* is a brown-black pigment widely distributed in nature both in plants and animals. In man and other mammals melanin is synthesized by special cells, melanocytes,[9] in the lowest layer of the epidermis, and the granules are deposited in the upper layers.

The concentration of melanin acts as a filter to prevent the sun's rays from penetrating to the dermal layer where blood vessels, nerves, and gland cells are located. Populations differ considerably in skin color, hence in their ability to endure direct exposure to the solar radiation for prolonged periods. The skin's blockage of ultraviolet radiation can also be accomplished by thickening of the corneum layer, which occurs in certain groups. The skin of many Mongoloid peoples has a thickened corneum packed with keratin, which gives the skin a yellowish color; this layer acts as an ultraviolet filter even though few melanin granules are present. In the dark skin of numerous Africans this layer is packed with melanin and filters out most of the ultraviolet. However, what is most significant for our investigation of human variability is the considerable range of difference in this filtering ability. Some African skin studied was heavily pigmented and filtered out about 95 percent of the ultraviolet; other samples blocked only about 50 percent. These results were due to variability in melanization of the skin as well as the thickness in the outer layer or corneum. Not only is the skin color in each population highly variable, but it changes during the lifetime of each individual. The skin is lighter in the newborn and darkens in the adult. These factors probably have important adaptative qualities, which will be considered in Chapter 5.

Variations in the concentration of melanin and its resulting filtering of the sun's rays have a very important consequence in altering the skin's ability to synthesize a very essential hormone-vitamin, *calciferol,* which is synthesized in the skin by the action of ultraviolet radiation on a steroid (7-dehydrocholesterol). These steroids lie in the epidermis below the

---

[9] The number of melanocytes is approximately the same in all races, and even albinos have a normal amount of these cells. Melanin differences must be due, then, to a difference in the activity of these cells, with the cells functioning at a high level in dark-skinned peoples, synthesizing large quantities of melanin, while in the fair-skinned northern Europeans the cells make very little melanin. However, the melanocytes in most people are stimulatd by ultraviolet radiation and will synthesize quantities of melanin in the presence of sunlight, which explains the ability of the lighter-skinned peoples to tan during the summer months. The tanning process is simply a buildup of melanin in the outer layers of the skin due to exposure to sunlight.

corneum layer, and there is no difference in the amount of these compounds (the pro-vitamin D) found in the skins of different races. The function of this hormone is essentially a regulation of the body's use of calcium and phosphorus; it controls absorption of calcium through the intestine, regulates renal excretion, and aids in skeletal mineralization. These functions are so critical that the lack of this hormone causes skeletal defects in children who suffer a deficiency (the skeletal malformation is called rickets). In the adult the vitamin D deficiency and the resulting calcium imbalance causes a reduction in mineralization of the skeleton (osteomalacia).

SOME BIOCHEMICAL CHARACTERISTICS

In a majority of the attempts to classify *H. sapiens* into subspecies the characteristics used were traits inherited in a rather complex way. Head shape, stature, skin color, and face form all are the result of a series of interactions between the environment and several genes. In short, they are polygenic traits whose exact mode of inheritance is not known; it is very difficult to differentiate between populations on this basis. However, there are some human phenotypes that are the result of inheritance of known gene combinations. These phenotypes, consisting of a large series of biochemical polymorphisms which can be detected by certain types of chemical tests, include the blood groups, several serum proteins, enzymes, hemoglobin, and the ability to taste or smell certain substances. The frequency of occurrence of certain of these substances in many populations varies widely, and they have been used as markers to differentiate between the groups. The following discussion lists some of the major markers useful in the study of human variability.

The Blood Groups

Blood consists primarily of the red blood cells (erythrocytes), which transport oxygen around the circulatory system, and the yellowish fluid part, or plasma. Plasma contains many elements vital to the proper functioning of the body, including *albumin,* blood clotting agents, and globulin fractions such as gamma globulin, which consists of antibodies whose responsibility is to defend the body against disease. In addition, there are white blood cells (leucocytes) and platelets, whose numbers are much less than the red cells. In case of injury or disease, however, the concentration of these cells may increase dramatically as part of the body's overall defense mechanism.

In addition to these components, there are substances that will cause the red cells from one person to agglutinate or clump together if they are mixed with serum (the plasma less fibrinogen) from certain other persons. Through a series of carefully controlled experiments, *Landsteiner,* a German serologist, found that the agglutination reaction, though it did not always occur, was frequent enough to make blood transfusions a very dangerous procedure. He worked out an explanation for these reactions between individuals that eventually became a description of three kinds of blood types in man, known as the ABO blood group.

Two substances are involved in this red cell-serum reaction, an *antigen* fixed to the surface of the red cell and a specific kind of *antibody* in the serum. An antigen, usually a large protein molecule attached to a sugar, has the ability to stimulate the production of antibodies, or it may react with an antibody already present in the system. Antibodies are also large protein molecules that are part of the gamma globulin of blood serum. Antibody-antigen reactions, in general, are a natural phenomenon in biological organisms, and a whole host of reactions take place constantly between individual organisms and the external world, especially when foreign substances such as bacteria, viruses, or foreign proteins are encountered.

The antigen can be thought of as a complex molecule with multiple combining sites or locations where antibodies are capable of connecting (Figure 3-4). The antibody, however, is a simpler structure which has only

FIGURE 3-4

Diagram of Antibodies-Antigen Reactions

Type   A   Cells

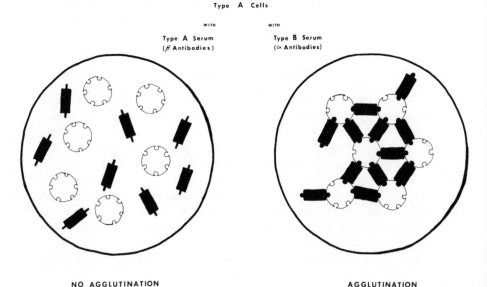

WITH   WITH

Type A Serum   Type B Serum
(β Antibodies)   (α Antibodies)

NO AGGLUTINATION   AGGLUTINATION

two combining sites. When the antibody connects with an antigen, there is
still a single site left which can connect with another antigen. In a reaction
between red-cell antigens and antibodies an antibody would bring together two red cells. This antibody-antigen reaction that occurs in blood
groups when different blood types are mixed is similar to the immune
response of the body against invading organisms: the reaction ultimately
makes it possible for the body's defense to destroy foreign substances or
to render them harmless.

The ABO Blood Group—This group of antigens is the best known
of a growing list of blood groups. The first one to be discovered, the ABO
has turned out to be one of the most important medically. Millions of
people have had their blood typed for this group since it was first discovered in 1900.

The ABO types are inherited by a simple Mendelian ratio (as noted
earlier). At first, there appeared to be three alleles which could determine
a person's blood type (ABO); two alleles were codominants and one was a
recessive. The genotype combinations listed determine a particular antigen (blood type) and also antibodies. These antibodies are normally
present in the person's serum, and their production does not have to be
stimulated by a foreign antigen.[10] The anti-A and anti-B antibodies are
probably determined by the same set of genes for the antigen.

Genotype	Phenotype (Blood Type)	Antibodies
AA } AO }	A	anti-B
BB } BO }	B	anti-A
AB	AB	none
OO	O	anti-AB

Comparison of ABO types in families, sometimes for three generations, has shown the exact mode of inheritance. Given the parental genotypes, the probable genotypes of the children can be predicted.

	1		2		3	
Parents	AB × OO	BB × OO		BO × AO		
Children	AO BO	BO BO	AB	AO	BO	OO

---

[10] These antibodies occur naturally, in contrast to a majority of the other
blood-group systems which have antibodies only when they are synthesized.

In mating 1, type O offspring are not possible, even though one parent has this blood type. Mating 2 produces only type B children. A mating of heterozygotes for type A and B produces four different blood types in their children, as shown in mating 3.

The genetics of the ABO system becomes more complex as additional alleles are detected. For example, there are actually two type A's, A_1 and A_2, which increase the number of alleles at the ABO locus to four.

The genes for ABO group are not evenly distributed throughout the world. Gene O is much more frequent than A or B, and some populations have mostly type O individuals; for example, the American Indians consist almost entirely of persons of type O blood. The gene for type A is the next most frequent; in small populations in relatively isolated areas, it

TABLE 3-9

Major Blood Group Systems [1]

System	Antigens	Genotypes	Phenotypes	Date of Discovery
ABO	A_1, A_2, B	OO, AA, BB, AB	O, A_1, A_2, B, AB	1900
Lewis	Le^a, Le^b	Le^aLe^a, Le^bLe^b, LeLe	Le (a+b−), Le (a−b+) Le (a−b−)	1946
Rh				
MNSs	N, N, S, s	MS/MS, MS/Ms, Ms/Ms, MS/NS, MS/Ns, Ms/NS, Ms/Ns, NS/NS, NS/Ns, Ns/Ns	M, N, MN, S, s, Ss	1927
P	P_1, P_2	P_1P_1, P_1P_2, P_2P_2, P_1p, P_2p, pp	P_1, P_2, p	1927
Lutheran	Lu^a, Lu^b	Lu^aLu^a, Lu^aLu^b, Lu^bLu^b	Lu (a+b−), Lu (a−b+)	1945
Kell	K (Kell) k (Cellano)	KK, Kk, kk	K+k−, k+k+, K−k+, (K−k−)	1946
Duffy	Fy^a, Fy^b	Fy^aFy^a, Fy^aFy^b, Fy^bFy^b, FyFy	Fy (a+b−), Fy (a+b+), Fy (a−b+), Fy (a−b−)	1950
Kidd	Jk^a, Jk^b	Jk^aJk^a, Jk^aJk^b, Jk^bJk^b	Jk (a+b−), Jk (a+b+) Jk (a−b+), Jk (a−b−)	1951
Diego	Di^a	Di^aDi^a, Di^aDi, DiDi	Di (a+), Di (a−)	1955
Sutter	Js^a	Js^aJs^a, Js^aJs, JsJs	Js (a+), Js (a−)	
Auberger	Au^a	Au^aAu^a, Au^aAu, AuAu	Au (a+), Au (a−)	1961
Xg	Xg^a	Xg^aY, XgY, Xg^aXg^a, Xg^aXg, XgXg	Xg (a+), Xg (a−)	1962

[1] Based on Buettner-Janusch, 1966, Giblett, 1969, and others.

reaches a high of around 50 percent and, together with type O, constitutes the majority of the ABO group. The allele B is the rarest of the ABO group; in some breeding populations it is totally absent. In Asia type B is more frequent than in Europe, where type A is highest.

Since the first description of the red-cell antigens of the ABO system over twenty other groups have been discovered. Table 3-9 lists the major groups together with the year of their discovery. Many of these, unlike the ABO system, have no naturally occurring antibodies. A majority of these systems are not important medically, since mixing them in blood transfusions has no apparent reactions. These antigen systems are usually of interest only to the human geneticist and anthropologist.

The Rh Blood Group—Perhaps second in importance to the ABO blood group system is the Rhesus system, which is often involved in a blood disease of the newborn, *erythroblastosis fetalis*. In this disease the red cells of the developing fetus are destroyed by antibodies made in the mother's blood in a response to certain antigens on the fetus red cells which the mother does not possess. Though the disease was known for many years, no explanation was possible until Landsteiner and Weiner in 1940 showed that anti-Rhesus serum [11] agglutinated red cells of some 85 percent of white New York patients tested. The 15 percent of the individuals who did not react to the serum were identified as Rhesus negative or Rh negative. About a year later the investigators discovered that mothers who gave birth to erythroblastosis infants were Rh negative (their blood cells did not react to the anti-Rhesus factor—see Figure 3-5).

Since the 1940s the many studies on the Rh factor have revealed that man possesses a large number of Rh antigen types which are inherited through Mendelian mechanisms. Two systems of notation have been worked out to describe the kinds of reaction to tests and mode of inheritance. One system, developed by Fisher and Race, is based on the concept that the reactions or potentials for the reactions are inherited as if they were determined by three closely linked loci, each with two alleles, each allele determining one antigentic response to an antiserum. The explanation by Weiner is founded on the assumption that there is only a single locus with eight allelic genes, each responsible for determination of an antigen which can combine with three or more kinds of antibodies.

Both these systems of notation are more complicated than the ABO because so many antiserum reactions have been determined. Fisher-Race notation uses Cc, Dd, Ee to represent the pair of alleles at each locus; the lower case does not indicate recessivity or dominance, since each allele determines the presence of an antigen, though an antibody for d has not

---

[11] Anti-Rhesus serum was produced by rabbits when they were injected with red cells from Rhesus monkeys.

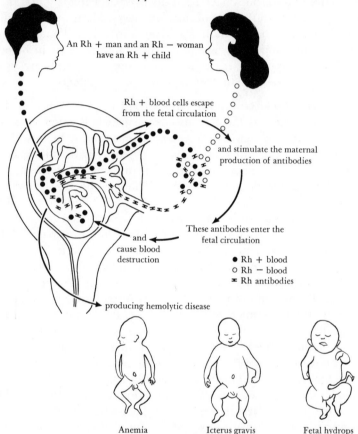

FIGURE 3-5

Diagram of Sensitization
of RH— Mother to RH+ Fetus

*[From McKusick, 1969; Redrawn from E. L. Potter, Rh: Its Relation
to Congenital Hemolytic Disease and to Intragroup Transfusion
Reactions (Year Book, 1947).]*

An Rh + man and an Rh — woman
have an Rh + child

Rh + blood cells escape
from the fetal circulation

and stimulate the maternal
production of antibodies

These antibodies enter the
fetal circulation

and
cause blood
destruction

● Rh + blood
○ Rh — blood
✖ Rh antibodies

producing hemolytic disease

Anemia   Icterus gravis   Fetal hydrops

been discovered yet. Since the three loci are so closely linked and crossover
is not known to occur, the loci are written together as a combination to
represent the genotypes. There are eight possible combinations, corresponding to the eight alleles postulated by Weiner. Both notation systems
are equally valid, though some immunologists prefer one over the other,
and both are used to indicate blood type in the Rh system. A typical
genotype might appear as

$$\frac{CDE}{cde}$$

this would show that all antigens in the systems are represented and would interact with the serum especially prepared for these tests.[12] The following chart shows the possible combination of alleles on the chromosome and the apparent mode of inheritance.[13]

Each parent in this example would test positive for C, but, since they are heterozygous for the alleles, one out of four offspring would be negative. The female, according to her genotype, is homozygous for gene d. She would not react to the anti-D serum test (this individual would be considered Rh negative). However, since her husband has the d and D genes, there is a 50 percent chance that a child produced by this mating would be Rh positive (possessing the D gene—see diagram). There would be a possibility, in this case, of the fetus stimulating anti-D antibody production in the maternal system. When such an event occurs, there is the risk of the fetus developing the erythroblastosis disease, because the anti-D antibodies from the mother's bloodstream easily cross through the placenta into the fetal circulation, where they agglutinate and then destroy the blood cells (see Figure 3-5). Naturally, if the genotype of the fetus is negative for D, there is no danger.

The genes for the Rh antigen system do not cause antibodies to be inherited, as in the case of the ABO system, which has naturally occurring

Male genotype	Female genotype
CDE / cde	Cde / cdE

Genotypes of offspring

gametes	Cde	cde
CDE	CDE / Cde	CDE / cdE
cde	cde / Cde	cde / cdE

[12] The Rh system is continually expanding as new antisera become available and new tests identify additional antigens. At present there are approximately 21 reagents used in testing the Rh groups.

[13] Genetic notation for both Fisher-Race and Wiener systems:

Allelic genes	*Antigen specificities*	*Three gene loci*
R^0	Rh_0, hr′, hr″	cDe
r′	rh′, hr″	Cde
r″	rh″, hr′	cdE
R′	Rh_1', (Rh_0, rh′, hr″)	CDe
R^2	Rh_2 (Rh_0, rh″, hr′)	cDE
R^Z	Rh_Z (Rh_0, rh′, rh″)	CDE
r^Y	rh_Y (rh′, rh″)	CdE
r	rh (hr′, hr″)	cde

antibodies. Theoretically any of the six antigens has a potential to stimulate antibody production, but only the D, C seems to cause trouble in the incompatible pregnancies described above. Some incompatibility between the parents also occurs in the case of the ABO blood-group system, which will be considered in Chapter 5.

The *MN* system was first discovered in 1928 when Landsteiner and Levine were able to prepare two types of antiserum against human red cells which would identify three types of individuals.[14] The symbols M and N were used to describe the genotypes of this new system. Inheritance of MN type appeared to be of this kind:

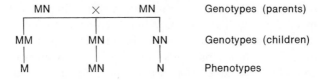

These alleles are codominants and each determines a characteristic response to antiserum. The heterozygote (MN) individual would react with both antisera and would distinguish this individual from the persons who react only with anti-M or anti-N. Unlike the ABO or the Rh systems, the MN system does not appear to have any medical importance—probably because no antibodies are known to occur in man (the antiserum used in the test is synthesized by injecting red cells into rabbits). Antibodies neither occur naturally (the genetically determined ones as in the case of the ABO blood group) or are induced (as in the Rh system).

An antigen closely linked to the MN locus is referred to by the term S. There appear to be only two alleles at this locus, Ss, with S dominant, so there are three genotypes: SS, Ss, ss. Both SS and Ss would be positive to the anti-S test, while s would not react to the antiserum. The S and the MN loci are linked so closely that there are no known cases of crossover. This means, as in the Rh system, that the genes are transmitted as a unit: MS, NS, and so on.

The interesting aspect of the MNS system is its even distribution among most of the world's peoples. Major exceptions in M and N frequencies are seen in the American Indians, who have a high frequency of alleles MS and Ms, and Australian Aborigines, who have extremely high frequencies of N, especially Ns. The significance of these distributions, though interesting, has yet to be determined.

---

[14] Many of the blood-group systems have been discovered by mixing blood cells with antiserum made from plant extracts or with antihuman serum made by injecting human red cells into certain animals, usually rabbits.

Minor Blood Groups—In addition to the major blood groups considered above, a number of other red-cell antigens systems have been identified (Table 3-9). These are inherited, and many are probably controlled by a single pair of alleles. They seem to be of little importance clinically, and so far they are of interest only to the geneticist; since many of these antigen systems occur more frequently in some of the world's peoples then in others, he uses them as gene markers to estimate population relationships or group distance. Blood groups like the Duffy and the Diego have proven especially useful because of their distinct distribution.

The Duffy blood group provides an effective method of determining Caucasian admixture in American Negroes (see Reed, 1969). The Fy^a allele is almost totally lacking in West and Central African populations, while it has a frequency of approximately 40 percent in Caucasian populations. American Negroes show varying frequencies of this allele (Table 3-10). This means the largest number of Fy Fy genotypes apparently exist

TABLE 3-10
Frequency of Duffy Allele Fy^a in Various Populations [1]

Population	Frequency of Fy^a allele (percent)
Africa	
Upper Volta	0%
Dahomey	0
Ghana	0
Nigeria	0
Kenya	
Kamba	0
Giryama	9.5
Bechuanaland	
Bushman (Central)	27.9
Bushman (Pooled sample)	31.2
South West Africa	
Bushman	15.7
Hottentot	27.9
Republic of South Africa	
Bantu	11.8
Congo	
Bantu	7.8
North America	
Negro	21–26
White	43

[1] Based on Hiernaux, 1966, and Reed, 1969.

in Africans, but many more populations need to be surveyed to establish the worldwide distribution.

The *Diego* group, originally discovered in Venezuelan Indians, has proven to be an "American Indian" gene. It also occurs in a few east Asian populations and a few Papuan populations in New Guinea. It is absent in Europeans, Africans and Eskimos. However, few population surveys have been made to establish a distribution.

The *Lutheran* blood group system has not yet proved useful for population studies, as a majority of the world's peoples are Lu^b (0.96 in Caucasoid, 0.97 in Negroid, and 1.0 in Mongoloid tests). Tests thus far have shown that only the two alleles Lu^a, Lu^b exist, though Lu (a—b—) have been discovered in a single family. The main interest this system has is its possible autosomal linkage to the secretor locus.

The *Lewis* blood group system is apparently under simple genetic control, probably by a single pair of alleles, Le^a, Le^b or Le, le. The major interest in this group is that it interacts with the secretor system and influences the presence of soluble antigens of the ABO system (see below). Allele Le is dominant to le and is responsible for the presence of Le^a substance in the blood. This substance interferes with the secretion of ABH [15] substances in the watery secretions of the body, and persons who are Le^a+ are nonsecretors. The interactions are complex, however, and influenced by alleles at the secretor locus. The Le allele has a frequency of 0.82 in Caucasoid, 0.32 in Negroid and 0.76 in Mongoloid groups tested.

Soluble antigens—A pair of allelic genes determine whether or not ABH blood-group substances are secreted in saliva and other watery secretions of the body such as tears, semen, milk, urine, and gastric juices. These alleles are known as the secretor genes (Se and se). If a person's genotype is Se se or Se Se, an ABH group antigen that is water soluble will be found in these bodily fluids.

Genotype	Phenotype
Se Se	
Se se	Secretor
se se	Nonsecretor

---

[15] When the ABO blood group was first studied it was assumed that O type was simply the absence of antigens determined by either A or B alleles. Further study demonstrated that there were certain antisera that would react with type O blood, and probably an antigen was present; this antigen was designated type H. It is apparently part of the A and B antigens as well, since cells from persons of type A or B will react with anti-H but less strongly than cells from a type O person. The order of strengths of reactions is O $>$ A$_2$ $>$ B $>$ A. This H substance is identifiable in the saliva, also a person having it is a secretor; hence the terminology ABH-soluble antigens.

The type of antigen secreted will be similar to the type on the surface of the red blood cell; that is, if a person's red-cell antigen is type A, then he will have the equivalent soluble antigens in his bodily fluids. The total interactions between the H-factor, Lewis group, and secretor genes are outlined in Table 3-11. While a majority are secretors, there are some differences; Europeans and persons of European ancestry have the greatest numbers of nonsecretors and Lewis positive.

Since few studies have been made, little information is available on the distribution of secretors. But the record to date indicates that most American Indians are secretors, while the majority of nonsecretors are in populations south of the Sahara. The two alleles are approximately equal in frequency in England, since there are about 25 percent nonsecretors.

The adaptive significance of these soluble antigens is not known, but some relationship to the digestive tract is likely, because they probably interact with the large number and variety of macromolecules which enter the digestive region daily in the form of food particles and bacteria. These antigens may in some way act as a part of a protective device to eliminate certain macromolecules that may be harmful to the system (see Otten, 1967).

ABNORMAL HEMOGLOBINS
AND OTHER RED-CELL VARIANTS

Hemoglobin is a complex molecule that makes up to 90 to 95 percent of the protein content of the human red blood cell. It is a complex of four polypeptide chains, two alpha chains of 141 amino acids each and two beta chains with 146 amino acids. Each of these long polypeptide chains

TABLE 3-11

Six Phenotypes Determined by
Bombay, Secretor, and Lewis Loci

		Antigens or Red Cells			Specificities Detectable in Saliva		
		ABH	Le(a)	Le(b)	ABH	Le(a)	Le(b)
H • Se •	Le•	+	−	+	+	[+] *	+
H•sese	Le•	+	+	−	−	+	−
H•Se•	Iele	+	−	−	+	−	−
H•sese	Iele	+	−	−	−	−	−
hh (Se or sese)	Le•	−	+	−	−	+	−
hh (Se or sese)	Iele	−	−	−	−	−	−

*Small amount of Le(a).

contains an iron molecule within a *heme group;* the major function of the iron is to combine with two oxygen atoms. This heme group gives blood its red color.

Hemoglobin has been the most thoroughly investigated of any protein molecule, and a large number of variant forms of this molecule have been found. Many of these variants—or abnormal hemoglobins—are inherited as single-gene traits, others have a more complex mode of inheritance. Certain of these variants will cause metabolic diseases, such as *sickle-cell anemia* or *thalassemia.* However, the red blood cell also contains enzyme systems which aid the hemoglobin in its major function: the transport of oxygen. A large number of hemoglobin forms may exist, while the red blood cell still maintains its respiratory function.

The sequence of the amino acids in each of the chains of hemoglobin provides it with a certain identity which is changed if any amino acid is replaced by another. For example, studies over the past few years have revealed many types of hemoglobin in man. Most of them usually differ only in a single amino acid in the beta chains. This simple substitution causes the hemoglobin to behave differently, and in certain cases the oxygen-delivering capacity is diminished. Some substitutions alter the entire character of the hemoglobin, as in the case of the sickle-cell substitution. The substitution of valine for glutamic acid produces a type of molecule that distorts the shape of the red cell when a quantity of oxygen is removed. The new shape that the cell assumes is often cresent or sickle-like. Frequently, changes in amino-acid sequences shorten the life of the red blood cell, which reduces the number in circulation. A most severe form of hemoglobin abnormality appears to be that caused by the sickle-cell substitution—hence the name *sickle-cell anemia.*

These hemoglobin variants all appear to be due to a single substitution of an amino acid. Family studies have shown that these substitutions are determined as a single-gene mechanism. Some of the principle variants are S, E, and C. If Hb^A is taken as the normal hemoglobin, then the genotype for some of the variant combinations are written as follows:

The majority of the cells would sickle in the individual with the SS combination, while the AS would be a carrier of the abnormal gene. This heterozygote can be identified by a simple test that chemically removes oxygen is removed. The new shape that the cell assumes is often crescent shape to be formed. The AS individual has a combination of normal and abnormal hemoglobin in all his red cells, and under most circumstances the cells will function properly. It is only under conditions where the demand for oxygen by the tissues is increased and a quantity is removed from the cell, as in vigorous exercise, that a certain number of these cells will undergo distortion. The distorted cells may then be destroyed and the total number in circulation reduced.

Distribution

Several hemoglobin types are distributed unevenly around the world, occurring with greater frequency in certain populations (Figure 4-4). The best-known distribution is that of Hb^S, which is found in populations throughout the middle part of Africa, around the Mediterranean, and among a few groups in eastern Turkey and in parts of India. This gene was once thought to be peculiar to African Negroes, but it has since been found widely distributed in many populations of the world (see Chapter 5 for further discussion). The E type hemoglobin has a much more limited distribution and reaches its highest frequency in India. Other regions of high frequency of type E also exist in Southeast Asia and New Guinea. Abnormal hemoglobins are not found in the New World except in persons who are descendants of African slaves and among a few others who have migrated from areas where these hemoglobin types are found. No hemoglobin abnormality is known to exist in native peoples of the New World.

Thalassemia, another type of hemoglobin abnormality, often results in anemia (Cooley's Anemia). Here, rather than there being a single substitution of an amino acid, the synthesis of either polypeptide chain is impaired. When beta-chain synthesis is retarded, this condition results in hemoglobin with a surplus of alpha-chain peptides. The reverse is true when alpha-chain synthesis is blocked: an excess of beta polypeptides will result. Each appears to be under the control of genes at different loci. Persons homozygous at one or the other locus will have a severe form (Thalassemia major), while the heterozygote will have a much milder form (Thalassemia minor).

Thalassemia major, owing to the high rate of destruction of red blood cells, produces a severe form of anemia. Afflicted individuals cannot survive unless blood transfusions are made regularly. Despite this severe selection Thalassemia is widespread throughout most of the Old World (Figure 3-6). The trait is probably due to codominant alleles, and these alleles exist in rather high frequencies in many populations. In certain regions of Italy 35 percent of the people have some form of Thalassemia, and in many Southeast Asia groups the gene frequency exceeds 15 percent. Possible explanations for these distributions and the probable environmental relationships will be considered in Chapter 5.

FIGURE 3-6

Distribution of Thalassemia and G6PD

(Redrawn from Buettner-Janusch, 1966)

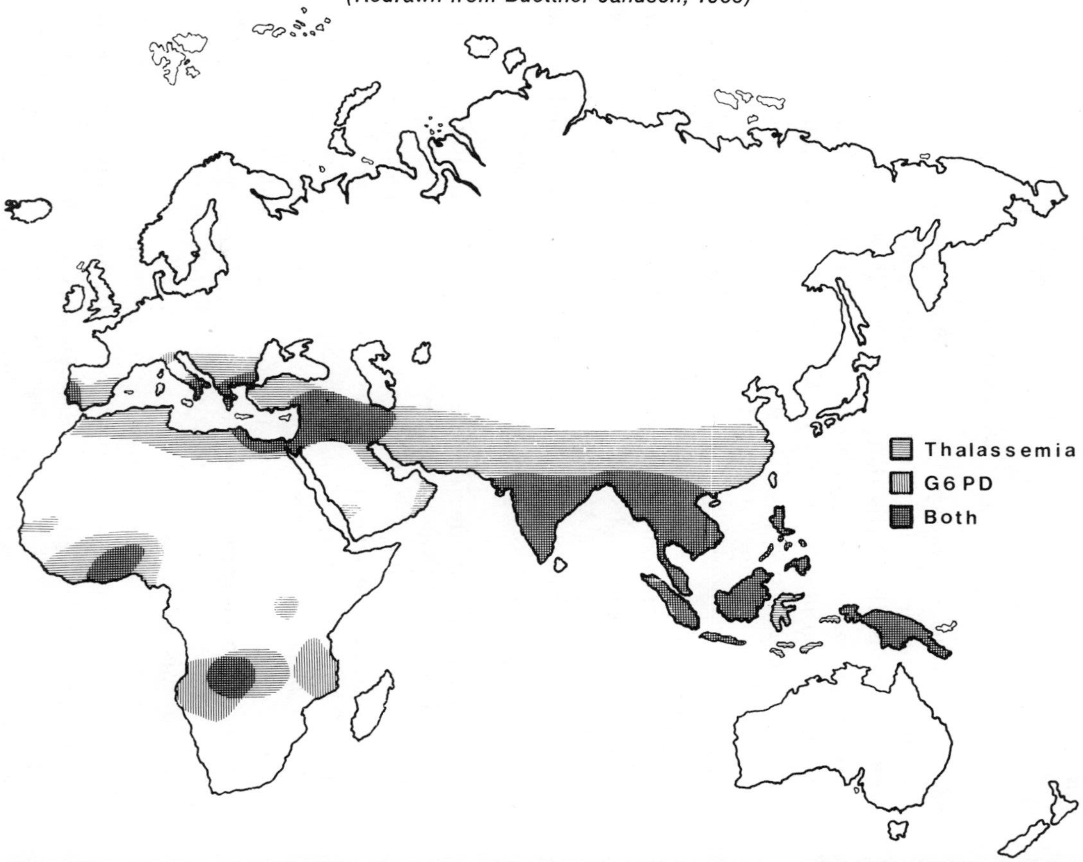

Thalassemia
G6PD
Both

G6PD Deficiency

Other red cell defects may result in anemia. Among these is an inherited condition where less than the normal activity of an enzyme—glucose 6 phosphate dehydrogenase, G6PD—exists in the red blood cells. Numerous people in the world are deficient in this enzyme, which serves an important function in the cell's metabolism. When they are exposed to certain substances [primaquine (an antimalarial drug) and fava beans], a number of their red cells may be destroyed. The consequent anemia will be corrected when the source of the irritant is removed and the body has time to replace the lost cells with new ones.

Such anemia, familiar for many years in several Mediterranean countries, is called *Favism* because of its apparent connection with fava beans, which are a dietary staple in many of these countries. Association with certain antimalarial drugs was made later. The exact nature of the deficiency was determined in the late 1950s when laboratory tests were developed to identify susceptible individuals. These persons had significantly less G6PD activity than those whose cells did not lyse under the test procedures.

Deficiencies in G6PD occur more frequently in males than females, which suggests that the synthesis of the enzyme G6PD is under the control of an x-linked gene. The G6PD variants exists in many populations from New Guinea to India and the countries of East Asia. The highest frequency of G6PD deficiency, however, exists in countries around the Mediterranean, particularly among Egyptians and people on the island of Sardina.

Finally, these red-cell variants—abnormal hemoglobins, G6PD deficiency, and Thalassemia—do not appear to be confined to a single geographical area nor are they unique to a particular "racial" group. The genes are widespread throughout many of the world's peoples and seems to follow the distribution of malaria. No explanation of migration and admixture has been able to account completely for these distributions. Movements of world's peoples have undoubtedly been involved, but other factors are also important, as will be shown in Chapter 5. It can be concluded here, though, that a particular gene should not be used as a marker of a person's racial affinity.

PROTEIN POLYMORPHISMS
AND INBORN ERRORS IN METABOLISM

Besides hemoglobins, a number of proteins in man (about 30 percent) are polymorphic. Their synthesis is under genetic control and when mutation occurs the protein changes its structure slightly—a condition similar to that in the hemoglobins. Several of these protein polymorphisms have been discovered in man's blood serum by techniques known as electrophoresis, in which an electric field is applied across a medium through which the protein molecules can migrate. Several kinds of media have been used, the most common being starch gel, filter paper, and acrylamide. Each protein molecule, because of its size and atomic configuration, has a particular charge and will migrate a certain distance during a time period. By this method the different proteins in human serum can be separated.

Haptoglobins

Haptoglobins are serum proteins, part of the alpha$_2$-globulins in serum, and have the capacity to combine with free hemoglobin (hemoglobin that has been released into the plasma when a red blood cell lyses). This serves to prevent the hemoglobin from being lost through excretion in the kidneys. Three types of haptoglobin are known, each apparently under genetic control through the action of a pair of nondominant alleles. The genotypes and phenotypes would appear as:

Hp^1Hp^1:   Haptoglobin 1-1
Hp^1Hp^2:   Haptoglobin 1-2
Hp^2Hp^2:   Haptoglobin 2-2

The occurrence of different haptoglobins varies widely, as shown in Table 3-12. The highest frequency of Hp^1 appears in tropical populations. The adaptive significance is not yet clear, but it may be related to a type of environmental selection, since Hp^1 has a greater affinity for hemoglobin and hence a higher binding capacity. This may be an advantage in certain populations where hemolytic anemia is very high. Persons with Hb^sHb^e genotypes appear to benefit from Hp^1.

Transferrins

Another serum protein variant is a beta-globulin fraction of serum, which binds with iron. The transferrins serve to transport iron to the tissues as needed, especially bone marrow where hemoglobin is formed. They exist in at least seventeen forms (as determined by their mobility in electric field) and each seems to be under genetic control of a nondominant allele. These transferrin variants are arranged in three groups designated TfC, TfD, TfB.

These polymorphisms are distributed unevenly throughout the species, several populations having only a single type (Table 3-13). TfC is the most common, while TfB is not widely distributed. The meaning of

TABLE 3-12

Geographic Distribution of Hp^1 Gene
(After Giblett, 1969)

Population	Number Tested	Hp^1 Frequency
Europe		
Norway	1000	0.36
Sweden	1003	0.38
France	406	0.40
England	218	0.41
Scotland	100	0.36
Italy (So.)	752	0.32
Spain (Basques)	107	0.37
Poland	151	0.36
Africa (North)		
Nigeria: Yoruba*	99	0.87
Senegal	398	0.63
Africa (East)		
Uganda*	165	0.63
Africa (Central)		
Congo: Metropolitan	151	0.77
Tutsi	86	0.52
Pygmies*	125	0.40
Africa (South)		
Zulu	113	0.53
Zulu	116	0.53
Hottentot	59	0.51
Bushmen	113	0.29
Bushmen	125	0.31
Asia		
China: Hong Kong	122	0.39
China: Malaya	103	0.28
Thailand	682	0.24
Malaya	236	0.23
Japan	822	0.28
South India: Tamils	291	0.09
Todas	89	0.35
Pakistan	392	0.21
North America		
Alaska: Eskimos	418	0.30
Arizona Navajo	263	0.45
New Mexico Apache	98	0.59
Mexico (several tribes)	711	0.33–0.70
Mexico Lacandon	89	0.92
Central America		
Panama: Cuna	174	0.38
South America		
Surinam (hybrids)	253	0.67
Ecuador Quechua	192	0.78
Peru (7 tribes)	661	0.44–0.69
Bolivia Aymara	71	0.70
Brazil: Xavante	78	0.46

TABLE 3-12 (Cont.)

Population	Number Tested	Hp^1 Frequency
Pacific Islands		
Australian Aborigines		
North Queensland	100	0.18
North Queensland	493	0.17
New Guinea	82	0.66
Solomon Is.*	183	0.64
Philippines	293	0.38
Samoa	80	0.59
Tonga	200	0.60

* Hp^0 phenotype greater than 10 percent.

TABLE 3-13

Frequencies of Three Transferrin Groups
(After J. Buettner-Janusch, 1966)

Population	Number Tested	Frequency		
		Tf C	Tf B's (fast)	Tf D's (slow)
Asia				
India				
Tamil	291	1.000		
Toda	89	1.000		
Ceylon				
Sinhalese	159	0.988	$0.006 B_2 C$	$0.064 CD_1$
Tamil	140	1.000		
Veddah	64	0.890		$0.094 CD_1$ $0.016 D_1$
Japan	822	0.984	0.001 BC	0.015 CD
Africa				
Nigeria				
Habe	120	0.850		$0.150 CD_1$
Fulani	111	0.937		$0.063 CD_1$
Fulani	68	0.838		$0.147 CD_1$ $0.015 D_1$
Ibo	70	0.871		$0.129 CD_1$
Congo				
Nonmetropolitan	446	0.933		$0.067 CD_1$
Pygmy	121	0.934		$0.066 CD_1$
South Africa				
Hottentot	59	0.932		$0.068 CD_1$
Zulu	116	0.974		$0.026 CD_1$
Bushman	113	0.876		$0.115 CD_1$ $0.009 D_1$

this polymorphism for this iron-binding protein is not known, but there may be a difference in binding capacity. Such difference would make certain forms more efficient in some populations, as was suggested for haptoglobins.

Errors in Metabolism

Some of the most interesting genetic polymorphisms in man exist in the complex system of enzymes that regulate metabolic processes. If the enzyme is lacking, a metabolic defect usually results and some product (often a protein) is not synthesized, or at least not properly. The absence of the correct enzyme, with the resulting metabolic defect, is often inherited as a recessive allele. A number of these enzyme defects are described below.

Phenylketonuria (PKU) is caused by the inheritance of an autosomal recessive gene. Individuals homozygous for this allele are unable to metabolize an essential amino acid, phenylalanine, which occurs in nearly all proteins. The excess taken in through the diet that is not used for protein synthesis is normally oxidized into tyrosine. The homozygote recessives have a block in their metabolic pathway (see Figure 3-7) and large quantities, up to fifty times normal, of phenylalanine accumulate in the blood. Some of this excess is oxidized, through another pathway, to phenylpyruvic acid. This substance is toxic to the central nervous system, as is the elevated quantity of phenylalanine. If the two substances persist in the bloodstream they do severe damage to the brain. Untreated, the PKU individual will suffer severe mental retardation and his I.Q. will be significantly lower than normal; from 20 to 80 is the victim's usual I.Q. range.

Approximately one baby in ten thousand is born with this inherited metabolic defect, mostly of European parents. Norway, Sweden, and Denmark seem to have the highest frequencies, while the condition is extremely rare for non-Europeans. Gene frequencies of 0.014 have been calculated for Ireland, 0.004 for England; the few reported cases in Japan have provided an estimate of 0.0002. If the affliction is identified in infancy, a carefully managed diet low in phenylalanine can prevent brain damage. As a preventive measure many states now require that all infants be tested at birth.

The PKU defect is part of a series of biochemical steps (Figure 3-7). At certain of these steps other enzyme defects occur which are inherited as recessives. One of these is *alkaptonuria,* which causes alkaptones to be excreted in the urine. These cause an affected person's urine to turn black when exposed to the air. No severe effects result from this condition, at

FIGURE 3-7

Metabolic Pathway for Phenylalanine and Tyrosine
(From Lerner, 1968)

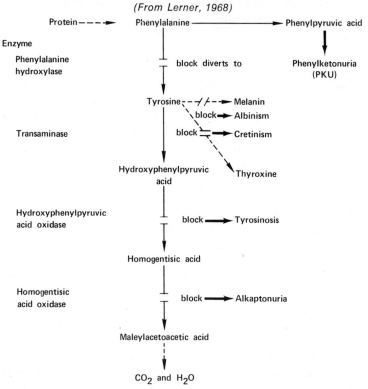

The first step in the metabolic breakdown of the essential amino acid phenylalanine is mediated by a liver-produced enzyme, phenylalanine hydroxylase. This enzyme is responsible for the substitution of an OH group for an H atom in phenylalanine, converting it to the amino acid tyrosine. Tyrosine, in turn, through a series of intermediate steps is converted into melanin, the skin pigment, and other substances. It is also broken down further along the pathway illustrated, in which the existence of intermediary steps is indicated by dotted arrows. If phenylalanine hydroxylase is absent, phenylalanine is in part converted into phenylpyruvic acid, which accumulates, together with phenylalanine, in the bloodstream. These substances are toxic to the central nervous system and lead to phenylketonuria. Other genetic metabolic defects in the tyrosine pathway towards oxidation are also known. As indicated in the diagram, absence of enzymes operating between tyrosine and melanin is the cause of albinism. Two other blocks illustrated produce tyrosinosis, a rare defect that causes hydroxyphenylpyruvic acid to accumulate in the urine, but requires no treatment, and alkaptonuria, which makes urine turn black on exposure to air, causes pigmentation to appear in the cartilage, and produces symptoms of arthritis. Another block in a different pathway, somewhat more complex, produces thyroid deficiency leading to goiterous cretinism.

least none comparable to those of PKU. However, darkly pigmented granules appear in the affected person's cartilage, and occasionally symptoms of arthritis result. This metabolic defect is rare, approximately one case in a million.

Lactase deficiency is now known to occur widely in *H. sapiens.* Most adults lack this enzyme, which is responsible for splitting milk sugar, lactose, into glucose and galactose. This condition may be inherited, but the genetic system has not been worked out as yet; possibly a recessive allele is responsible. The study of genetics is complicated by the possibility that lactase activity may be induced.

People who lack this enzyme, which includes a majority of Asians and Africans, are unable to tolerate fresh milk in their diet (Table 3-14). Normally, this is no handicap, since adults seldom consume fresh milk, even in populations who rely on cattle herding as a major means of subsistence. Usually milk is fermented first and eaten as a form of cheese. In this form, the bacteria have done the work of lactase and have split the milk sugar into products easily digested by the adult.

Galactosemia is due to a lack of the enzyme galactose-1-phosphate uridyl transferace. The major function of the enzyme is to metabolize

TABLE 3-14

Frequency of Lactase Deficiency [1]

Group	No. of Subjects	Percent Deficient
American Negro	97	74% (approx.)
Batutsi (Rwanda)	12	17
Bahina (Ankole)	11	9
Australian Aborigines		
Papunya (all less than 15 years old)	25	90
Maningrida (age range 6 to 48 months;		
mean 22 monthly)	19	80
Greenland Eskimos	32	72
American Indian (Chami, Colombia)	24	100
American Indian	3	67
Chinese	20	85
Formosa	(7)	
U.S.	(3)	
Philippines	(10)	
Baganda (Africa)	17	94
Bantu	35	89
Thai	140	97
Thai	75	100

[1] Based on McCracken, 1971.

galactose, one of the sugars that is produced when lactose is split. Afflicted individuals, if they survive infancy, become severely retarded in their growth and development. Inheritance is believed due to a recessive gene. The homozygote shows very little or no enzyme activity, while the parents, who are heterozygotes, have less than normal activity. Unfortunately, we do not have sufficient data to describe the distribution of this defect.

Taste Sensitivity—Perhaps no other polymorphism is so easily detected by a simple test as is taste sensitivity to a substance called *phenylthiocarbamide* or PTC. In high concentrations this substance tastes bitter to some people but not to others. Since the accidental discovery of this condition over thirty years ago, many millions of people have been tested and the frequency of tasters and nontasters calculated.

The ability to detect the substance PTC is determined by a dominant gene (T); persons who are TT or Tt can detect the bitter taste. In almost all populations tested there are tasters and nontasters, but as more careful tests have shown lately there are various degrees of sensitivity. The homozygote dominant individual (TT) tends to be a little more sensitive than the heterozygote (Tt) or the homozygote recessive (tt) and can detect the bitterness in more dilute solutions.

The frequency of the nontaster is shown in Table 3-15. We can see high frequencies of nontasters in several major racial divisions, so the frequency of the T gene does seem to be useful for sorting out groups of *H. sapiens*. Variations in taste sensitivity also exist in several subhuman primates; studies have reported taster variation in Chimpanzees and Rhesus (see Eaton and Gavan, 1965).

The significance of this polymorphism is not certain yet but there is some suggestion of a relationship between thyroid-gland activity and ability to taste PTC. The nontasters seem to be more susceptible to thyroid deficiency, and a higher frequency of nodular goiter is found among them than in tasters. Several plants of the Cruciferae family (cabbage, turnips, mustard greens, etc.) contain the thiocyanate group, which is responsible for the bitter taste in PTC. This substance is part of the thioglucosides, which can block iodine absorption of the thyroid gland under certain conditions. One hypothesis explaining the taster polymorphism is that tasters were able to reject plants containing substances which act as thyroid depressants.

BAIB (beta amino isobutyric acid) is an end product of pyrimidine metabolism (nucleic acid). Usually, catabolic processes continue until this, too, is broken down into end products, but in some individuals high levels of it are excreted in the urine. This high excretion rate is believed due to an autosomal recessive, but the condition apparently does not cause any metabolic defect as in the case of PKU and alkaptonuria.

TABLE 3-15

Frequency of Nontasters [1]

Population	Number Tested	Percent Nontasters
Formosan (Natives)	1,756	1.8
Cree and Beaver Indians (N. Alberta)	489	2.0
Ramah Navahoes	264	2.0
Chinese (in Malaya)	50	2.0
Africans, mostly West African	74	2.7
Bantu, Kenya	208	3.8
Aborigines (Senoi), Malaya	50	4
Lappish (Finland)	140	6.42
Japanese (Brazil)	295	7.11
Japanese (Japan)	656	8.23
Chinese (in London)	66	10.6
Negro (White admixture; Brazil)	534	12.83
Chilean	216	13.43
Jewish (North Africa)	340	15.00
Malays	50	15.6
Malayan	237	16.04
Northeastern Hindu (Riang)	401	16.21
"Cabocio" Brazil	258	16.28
Negritos, Malaya	50	18
Jewish (Ashkenazim; Europe)	440	20.68
Jewish (non-Ashkenazim; Balkan)	101	21.78
Northeastern Brazilians	296	23.31
Belgian	425	23.76
Portuguese	454	24.0
Spaniards, Northeastern	306	24.8
White (Italian admixture; Brazil)	74	24.32
Basques, Spain	98	25.0
Eskimos, N. Alaska	68	25.8
Arab (Sudan)	1,963	25.40
Tamils in Malaya	50	27.2
Finns	202	29.2
U.S. White	3,643	29.8
Hindu	256	29.30
Norwegians	266	30.5
White (Rio de Janeiro, Brazil)	164	30.49
Danes	314	31.8
Swedish	200	32.00
English (London)	541	32.90
Indian (Guajiro, Venezuela)	100	40.00
Eskimos, Labrador	130	41
Bombay Indians	200	42.5

[1] Based on Saldanha and Nacrur, 1963; Allison and Blumberg, 1959.

The presence or absence of BAIB does not appear to have any significance. Persons who are low excretors (less than 40 mg/day) do not seem to be any more or less fit than high excretors of (300 mg/day), and no disease correlations have been found. However, frequencies of high excretors vary widely (Table 3-16). Asians, judging from Chinese and Japanese samples, tend to have a large number of excretors, while American whites and Europeans in general tend to be low; around 10 percent are high excretors. The highest excretion rates are found in Micronesia. The meaning of this variant is not clear. It may simply be a transient polymorphism that does not interfere with fitness and is selectively neutral.

TABLE 3-16

Distribution of BAIB Excretors

(After Buettner-Janusch, 1966)

Population	Number Tested	Frequency of High Excretors
North America		
European descent		
Michigan	71	0.03
Texas	255	0.10
New York	218	0.10
New York	148	0.11
African descent		
Michigan	25	0.20
New York	38	0.15
Indians		
Apache	110	0.59
Apache	113	0.42
Eskimo	120	0.23
Chinese	33	0.45
Japanese	41	0.41
Central America		
African descent (Black Caribs)	285	0.32
Asia		
India	16	0
Thailand	13	0.46
Marshall Islands		
Rongelap	188	0.86
Utirik	18	0.83

RECOMMENDED READINGS AND LITERATURE CITED

ABBIE, A. A. 1967. "Book review: *The Living Races of Man*," *Current Anthrop.*, 8: 113–114.

ALLISON, A. C. and B. S. BLUMBERG. 1959. "Ability to taste phenylthiocarbamide among Alaskan Eskimos and other populations," *Human Bio.*, 31(4): 352–359.

BEALS, KENNETH L. 1972. "Head form and climatic stress," *Am. J. Phys. Anthrop.,* 37(1): 85–92.

BOYD, WM. C. 1963. "Four achievements of the genetical method in physical anthropology," *Am. J. Phys. Anthrop.,* 65: 243–252.

BRACE, C. LORING. 1962. "Cultural factors in the evolution of the human dentition," in *Culture and the Evolution of Man,* M. F. Ashley Montagu, ed. New York: Oxford University Press, pp. 343–354.

———. 1963. "Structural reduction in evolution," *The American Naturalist,* XCVII (892): 39–49.

BRACE, C. LORING, and PAUL E. MAHLER. 1971 "Post-pleistocene changes in the human dentition," *Am. J. Phys. Anthrop.,* 34: 191–204.

BUETTNER-JANUSCH, JOHN. 1966. *Origins of Man.* New York: John Wiley & Sons, Inc.

CARBONELL, VIRGINIA M. 1963. "Variations in the frequency of shovel-shape incisors in different populations," in *Dental Anthropology,* D. R. Brothwell, ed. Elmsford, N.Y.: Pergamon Press, pp. 211–233.

COMAS, JUAN. 1960. *Manual of Physical Anthropology.* Springfield, Ill.: Charles C Thomas, Publisher.

DAMON, ALBERT. 1965. "Stature increase among Italian-Americans: Environmental, genetic, or both?," *Am. J. Phys. Anthrop.,* 23: 401–408.

DOBZHANSKY, THEODOSIUS. 1962. *Mankind Evolving.* New Haven and London: Yale University Press.

EATON, JOHN W. and JAMES A. GAVAN. 1965. "Sensitivity to P-T-C among primates," *Am. J. Phys. Anthrop.,* 23: 381–388.

FRISCH, ROSE and ROGER REVELLE. 1969. "Variation in body weights and the age of the adolescent growth spurt among Latin American and Asian population, in relation to calorie supplies," *Human Biology,* 41(2): 185–212.

GIBLETT, ELOISE R. 1969. *Genetic Markers in Human Blood.* Philadelphia: F. A. Davis Co.

HARRISON, G. A., J. S. WEINER, J. M. TANNER, and N. A. BARNICOT. 1964. *Human Biology.* New York and Oxford, England: Oxford University Press.

HIERNAUX, J. 1966. "Peoples of Africa from 22° N to the Equator," in *The Biology of Human Adaptability,* Paul T. Baker, ed. Oxford: The Clarendon Press, pp. 91–110.

HOLLOWAY, RALPH L., JR. 1966. "Cranial capacity, neural reorganization, and hominid evolution: A search for suitable parameters," *Am. Anthrop.,* 68: 103–121.

———. 1966. "Cranial capacity and neuron number: A critique and proposal," *Am. J. Phys. Anthrop.,* 25: 305–314.

HULSE, FREDERICK S. 1967. "Selection for skin color among the Japanese," *Am. J. Phys. Anthrop.,* 27: 143–156.

KELSO, A. J. 1970. *Physical Anthropology.* Philadelphia, Pa.: J. B. Lippincott Co.

KROGMAN, WILTON M. 1971. "Book Review: *Compilation of Common Physical Measurements of Adult Males of Various Races.* Albert E. Casey and Eleanor L. Downey. *Physical Anthropology* (Reference Manual). Birmingham, Ala.: Amite & Knocknagree Historical Fund." *American Anthrop.,* 73: 442.

LERNER, MICHAEL I. 1968. *Heredity, Evolution and Society.* San Francisco: W. H. Freeman & Co., p. 91.

McCRACKEN, ROBERT D. 1971. "Lactase deficiency: An example of dietary Evolution," *Current Anthrop.,* 12(4–5): 479–500.

McKUSICK, VICTOR A. 1969. *Human Genetics.* Englewood Cliffs, N.J.: Prentice-Hall, Inc., p. 9.

MOLNAR, STEPHEN. 1971. "Human tooth wear, tooth function and cultural variability," *Am. J. Phys. Anthrop.,* 34: 175–190.

MONTAGU, M. F. ASHLEY. 1960. *An Introduction to Physical Anthropology.* Springfield, Ill.: Charles C Thomas, Publisher.

OSBORNE, R. H. and F. V. DE GEORGE. 1959. *Genetic Basis of Morphological Variation.* Cambridge, Mass.: Harvard University Press.

OTTEN, CHARLOTTE M. 1967. "On pestilence, diet, natural selection, and the distribution of microbial and human blood group antigens and antibodies," *Current Anthrop.,* 8: 209–219.

POTTER, E. L. 1947. "Rh: Its relation to congenital hemolytic disease and to intragroup transfusion reactions." Chicago: Year Book Medical Publishers, Inc.

PUTNAM, CARLETON. 1967. *Race and Reality.* Washington, D.C.: Public Affairs Press.

REED, T. EDWARD. 1969. "Caucasian genes in American Negroes," *Science,* 165: 762–768.

SALDANHA, P. H. and J. NACRUR. 1963. "Taste thresholds for phenylthiourea among Chileans," *Am. J. Phys. Anthrop.,* 21: 113–120.

SCHULTZ, A. H. 1926. "Fetal growth of man and other primates." *Quart. Rev. Bio.,* 1(4): 465–521.

TOBIAS, PHILIP V. 1970. "Brain-size, grey matter and race—Fact or fiction," *Am. J. Phys. Anthrop.,* 32: 3–26.

———. 1971. *The Brain in Hominid Evolution.* New York and London: Columbia University Press.

VON BONIN, G. 1963. *The Evolution of the Human Brain.* Chicago: University of Chicago Press.

WEYL, NATHANIEL and STEFAN T. POSSONY. 1963. *The Geography of Intellect.* Chicago: Henry Regnery.

WOLPOFF, MILFORD H. 1968. "Climate influence on the skeletal nasal aperture," *Am. J. Phys. Anthrop.,* 3: 405–424.

———. 1971. *Metric Trends in Hominid Dental Evolution.* Cleveland: Press of Case Western Reserve University, p. 70.

chapter four

Distribution
of
Human Differences

We have been using the term *race* in reference to groups or populations who share a common history and a large number of alleles—applying the term cautiously with full awareness of the confusion surrounding it and its multiple uses. Both *race* and *subspecies* are part of our vocabulary and can be applied effectively in discussions of human variation if used with a consistent meaning throughout; unfortunately, this consistency is lacking in many writings on human variation. It is not the purpose of this chapter to dispute what races are or are not, nor do we wish to enumerate supposed divisions of mankind; rather, we shall outline some methods of grouping species variability for purposes of study.

Race has been applied in reference to units as small as local breeding populations (demes) or to groups of populations occupying entire continents (such as the Negro race). Race has also been used quite frequently to describe a culturally or politically defined group (the Jewish, Aryan, English, and so on). Casual use of the phrase *the human race* is a literary convention, having nothing to do with biological classification. Also, in the various definitions discussed earlier, geographical, local, and microgeographical races are described. Certain of these groups are small local breeding populations which contain a few hundred individuals; others are major, geographically defined divisions. Further confusion is added by the use of different characteristics as sorting criteria.

The question of how the human species should be divided for description and study is a difficult one, particularly since racial differences are trivial in comparison to species differences, and the majority of human alleles are shared by all large population groups. These factors, together with the reality of population variability, has caused several biologists to abandon the race concept as a viable biological tool. Hiernaux (1964: 43), for example, observes: "In my opinion, to dismember mankind into races as a convenient approximation requires such a distortion of the facts that any usefulness disappears."

There is general agreement, however, that an understanding of human variation is basic to comprehending human adaptation. Some workers consider racial classification a means of studying adaptation and thus a useful tool; others dismiss race as but an artifact of man's past. Many believe that traits should be considered individually and not as a group or cluster unless the resulting classification, based on one character, reflects the variability of others (Livingstone, 1964: 47).

Regardless of one's definition or application of the concept, we should remember the point raised earlier: there is no reason to assume there is now, or ever has been, a *fixed number* of races. If we keep this in mind, we can avoid the trap that so many nineteenth-century naturalists fell into: "If races change, how do races come to be?" This logical impasse retarded the study of human biology for many generations. In fact, we are only now beginning to appreciate the complexity of our very polytypic species, whose variability is a result of a series of interactions between the social and biological systems.

Human variability as it is distributed through time and space depends upon a multitude of factors. Several are the same factors that operate on any biological population, as discussed in Chapter 2. But man is mobile and can manipulate the environment, and these abilities affect the elaboration of complex social systems which regulate behavior extensively, particularly breeding behavior. The establishment of abstract boundaries or mating circles and the custom of excluding outsiders are strong factors in directing gene flow, determining the shape of the new generation in an increasingly nonrandom way.

The history of a population—how long it has lived in a given area, what selective forces have been acting on it, and what contacts it has had with other populations—help determine the distribution of human variability. The effects of the European colonization dramatize the significance of mass movements of people. Smaller-scale, more gradual changes can also occur through interpopulation contact and through the establishment of sedentary populations, both occurring as consequences of new technology or subsistence patterns such as agricultural activities.

If we take into account these factors that influence the distribution of our species, then any grouping of human variability into units, populations, races, or subspecies becomes a much more viable means of studying human diversity. The way in which we chose to group human populations depends, of course, on our purpose. We must keep this purpose in mind when working with these groups. For example, one should not establish races or ethnic units on the basis of sociopolitical criteria and then explain or interpret their existence in biological terms. The same stricture applies to groups established on the basis of geographical boundaries. The so-called natural boundaries do not prevent interpopulation contact, though distance does, of course, reduce gene flow.

Human differences are distributed in some rather interesting patterns around the world. If we take a single trait or several traits together, we see that many population groups vary widely. The worldwide distribution of traits such as the ABO blood group, Rh blood group, abnormal hemoglobin, or the gene for taste sensitivity to phenyltiocarbamide show quite a wide difference between many populations. The fact remains, however, that these populations have been established because of conditions other than their gene frequencies. The combinations of genes in these populations are found there because of social, geographical, and cultural conditions that have constructed and maintained the biological unit which can be defined as a breeding population.

RACE AS A BIOLOGICAL UNIT

Explaining the arrangement of the varieties of organisms found in the natural world is as much a problem today as it always has been. With the newer techniques of taxonomy which utilize computer facilities investigators can process many thousands of items of information, many more than could the naturalists of earlier periods. But rather than clarifying and establishing definite boundaries between populations, this additional information raises new questions and often casts doubt on the validity of many older, accepted taxonomic units.[1]

The problem is not whether the earlier groupings were a true, accurate description of nature. The former methods merely had another way of looking at biological diversity, especially in the characteristics that were measured and considered significant at that time. Since the development of genetical theory and the description of DNA, life is now seen quite differently. Groups of organisms appear as dynamic units, many of whose characteristics change from generation to generation. Types or

[1] For further discussion see Ehrlich and Holm, 1962, Ehrlich and Raven, 1969, and Mayr, 1963.

averages are no longer considered a sufficient means to describe groups of individuals participating in a breeding population. It is this dynamic condition that makes it extremely difficult to establish any all-inclusive taxonomic unit. The older definitions of species as elementary units which are determined when collections of animals are sorted into groups are sufficient only as a first step. Even the description of a species as a reproductive unit, genetically isolated, has many exceptions when animals are studied under new conditions brought about by a change in habitats. Thus, other organisms present taxonomic problems as well as man.

The study of human diversity, especially the attempts to sort man into subspecies or races, is hampered by the disagreement over several aspects of this diversity: its origin, its relation to the environment, and whether or not basic racial stocks are "real" and of great antiquity. Species are natural biological units held together by gene flow (Ehrlich and Raven, 1969: 1228), while subspecies divisions are made on strictly an arbitrary basis, and such vague criteria as a 75 percent rule are employed —a "good" subspecies is one in which 75 percent of the individuals, examined can be recognized as belonging to that group. However, the number of individuals of a subspecies that we cannot classify often exceeds those that we can (Abbie, 1963: 192).

Subspecies are considered as a grouping of individuals or populations who share a number of characteristics in common—no single one being sufficient to differentiate between subspecies. Races then might be described as a group of populations who share a close common ancestry and who have been subjected to similar selective forces. The existence of such conditions would result in a high degree of similarity between the genetic systems of these population groups. The concept of race becomes much more useful if considered merely as a grouping of populations (see Hiernaux, 1964: 33). In previous discussions various definitions were listed for race, and these definitions took into account the many racial differences which appear to relate to geographical histories of each group. Dobzhansky stated (1944: 252): "It is recognized that most living species are more or less clearly differentiated into geographic races, each race occupying a portion of the species distribution area."

The importance of geography has often been recognized in the definition of races. Garn (1961) used spatial distribution of human varieties as a means of establishing racial groups. He provided us with geographical, local, and micro races (discussed earlier, p. 17). Microgeographical races and local races are smaller, less inclusive groups, comparable to the breeding populations used by many workers who study human variation. These basic units are subject to localized natural selection, and population size is also effective in causing differentiation between groups. The largest, most inclusive group—the geographical race—includes many diverse local groups. In a way this category is misleading, because often members of geographical races share only a few physical attributes. The geographical race conforms most closely to the older description of basic racial stocks or major races (usually the three—Mongoloid, Caucasoid, and Negroid).

Except for a superficial identification of the majority of the inhabitants of a continent, "basic stock" or "geographical race" tells us little about biological diversity or the interrelationships between breeding populations or the effects of the environment, which are the dimensions of the selective forces which act on the populations. "Basic stock" reveals little about gene combinations. "Geographical race" is merely a convenient label applied in a broad sense. In order to describe and study human variability, we must use a more restricted and precise grouping, because otherwise important differences will be obscured.

Many characteristics show a disrespect for classical, time-honored boundaries. This was recognized a number of years ago; Hooton (1936: 512), for example, observed: "There exists no single physical criterion for distinguishing race; races are delimited by the association in human groups of multiple variations of bodily form and structure." Another factor illustrated by these diagrams is that race or any such label used to identify human groups is nothing more than an informational abstraction which provides us with a research tool to investigate biological variability (see Baker, 1967: 21). Such labels have no more reality than any others that we use to identify objects we encounter in our environment. Such an approach has often been refuted, and declarations have been frequent that there is no such thing as race.

What causes this diversity of our species? Several sources have been described. First, independent or special creation has been widely advanced as an explanation. This theory, assuming multiple parallel lines of evolution, must contend with numerous gaps in the fossil record. Also, the argument that diverse populations have been linked together by gene flow and hence have maintained species continuity makes it difficult to support independent parallel evolutionary lines. "The presence of intermediates is presumptive evidence that the extreme races are united by gene flow through the intermediate links, and, therefore, are unlikely to be isolated from each other reproductively." (Dobzhansky, 1944: 253)

Another explanation of human diversity is that differing forces of natural selection caused the formation of relatively distinct groups. Before Darwin's theory of natural selection was published, a number of authors described the effects of climate and food on man and suggested that these factors may have contributed to human variation. Buffon, for example, observed in 1791: "Three causes . . . must be admitted, as concurring in the production of those varieties which we have remarked among the different nations of this earth: (1) the influence of climate; (2) food, which has a great dependence on climate; and, (3) manners, on which climate has, perhaps, a still greater influence."

We must consider yet a third factor, the fact that human differences —especially those often used to establish racial groups—are not as extreme or as great as generally supposed. In fact, for a few characteristics, differences between male and female are sometimes greater than differences between races. The tendency often is to exaggerate human variation, or in certain cases to be misled by similarities of a few characteristics. For example, Canary Islanders were thought to have a major Negro component in their makeup—an assumption based on morphological studies. More recent studies of haptoglobins and dermatoglyphics show little indication of such affinity, raising doubts about there being major Negroid elements in the populations.

Intraracial variation is, in some groups, very great indeed but often overlooked. An example is the diversity found in the American Indians (Boyd, 1963). A brief glance at the accompanying tables and photos reveals a wide diversity throughout the native peoples of the western hemisphere (Figure 4-1). No single characteristic of any group suffices to describe the "typical" Indian. African peoples are another example: it is not a continent populated by a homogeneous race, no matter how the division is made (see Hiernaux, 1966).

The principal causes of raciation are usually considered to be isolation, population size, and natural selection in the local area of habitation. With the semiisolation of a breeding population or, rather the reduction of gene flow, few new genetic materials are introduced, and the

TABLE 4-1
Stature of Some American Indians [1]

Tribe	Location	Stature (cm) (Males)
Motilon	Brazil	146.2
Jivaro	Brazil	154.2
Maya	Yucatan	155.4
Otomi	Southern Mexico	158.0
Hopi	Arizona	161.1
Zuni	New Mexico	161.4
Navaho	New Mexico	169.6
Aymara	Chile	161.8
Eskimo	St. Lawrence Island	165.0
Yaqui	Sinola	166.7
Papago	Arizona	168.8
Choctaw	Canada	171.4
Pima	Arizona	171.8

[1] Based on Comas, 1960, and Newman, 1953, and others.

FIGURE 4-1

Photos of
Five American Indians

1. Umatilla Chief of Eastern Washington. 2. Man from Rio Yasa tribes of Venezuela. 3. Karaja Indian of Brazil. 4. Papago of Southern Arizona. 5. Hoopa Indian of Northern California. *All courtesy of the American Museum of Natural History.*

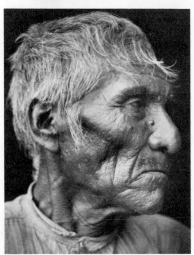

local selective forces have an opportunity to exert maximum selection. Certain gene combinations then can accumulate. However, some biologists feel that the importance of gene flow has been exaggerated. In an article discussing population differentiation, Ehrlich and Raven (1969) describe the relative influences of gene flow and natural selection. They stress that the issue of speciation or population differentiation is by no means settled; in some species gene flow is important as a factor in preventing differentiation, but in most it is not.

Because of man's wider-ranging activities and his ability to adapt to most areas of the earth, gene flow probably plays an important role in maintaining similarity throughout the species. Much of man's diversity seems to have been overstressed, and many of these differences are usually rather superficial. More significant than the differences are the similarities. Though race or subspecies is considered by many to be the first stage of speciation, it must be remembered that genetic variability within human populations is essentially equivalent to genetic variation between them. Because of human polymorphism, mankind cannot be subdivided into one group with zero percent and one group with 100 percent frequency of any one characteristic (except for a very few monogenic traits), which makes it very difficult to establish taxonomic units. Race, or subspecies, has been referred to as an artifact of evolution, and it is not the unit that evolution acts on (Mayr, 1963: 349). Further, classification by itself does not produce new knowledge; it is only a mental operation performed on existing knowledge (Hiernaux, 1964: 34). If these statements are indeed true, then what is the unit that evolution acts on and what is the most functional unit to investigate when studying human diversity?

BREEDING POPULATIONS

The most suitable units for study are smaller local populations, groups of intermarrying persons whether tribes, castes, or inhabitants of a particular region. (Hiernaux, 1971: 40)

Earlier we defined breeding population as a group of actually or potentially interbreeding individuals. This general definition fits most sexually reproducing organisms, but man in many ways is unique. His elaborate social organization and culturally directed behavior make the human breeding population a unique result of the interaction of multiple biological and behavioral forces. Because of man's *behavior,* the total genome of the species is distributed in space in clustered units.

Human mating patterns determine which individuals produce the next generation. A complex of social customs and taboos proscribe and prescribe sexual relations and establish the basis for family life as well as family lineages, clans, caste systems, and religious affiliations; these present culturally defined boundaries that in turn effect the gene combination of the next generation.

An example of how social systems determine gene frequency can be seen in the case of the x-linked recessive gene which causes an individual to be deficient for G6PD (see page 35). In patrilocal-patrilineal societies where males remain in the community and bring in brides from outside, many of the x-linked genes are lost, since two-thirds of the x chromosomes are provided by the female in any population. In this case the G6PD-deficient gene will be scarcer in a patrilocal community, because the daughters of G6PD-deficient males will leave, taking the gene with them, and the women moving into the community will probably come from a group that lacks the recessive trait (see Giles 1962). The converse, when the society is matrilocal (males marrying out of the community), maintains any x-linked gene at a higher rate. These examples show how society can direct gene exchange, which in turn causes change in gene frequencies. It is extremely important, then, to understand the functioning of a group as a social unit when one studies their genetic composition.

Geographical distance is another important consideration, for it obviously limits mating choices. In prehistoric times and even among primitive peoples today distance was a major restriction to gene flow. In modern societies, as recorded by Brierley (1970: 69), a man used to find his mate within 600 yards of his residence, but when the bicycle was invented the average distance jumped to 1,600 yards. If this increase in distance seems impressive, one has only to consider the mobility that has been brought about by invention and wide use of the automobile. As modern transportation has increased mobility further still, a broader exchange of genes is to be expected. Where formerly small breeding units were restricted by economics, politics, or geography to a village community, today the mating circles have expanded and the gene pool is much broader.

In more complex societies with caste and stratification, economic, religious, or political groupings, social distance plays a role similar to geographic distance. Peasant-aristocracy stratification in medieval Europe tended to isolate breeding populations and cluster genetic units within smaller areas. A similar situation exists even today in Latin America, and the persistence of rigid caste systems as in India or in the peasant societies in Latin America establishes an immense social distance between groups. The "untouchable" in India has no chance of mating with the higher-caste Brahman, for the Brahman would have to suffer severe religious sanctions. Religious enclaves also have proven effective in isolating their populations from the surrounding community. The Amish and Dunkers of Pennsylvania have significantly different gene frequencies for traits such as the blood groups. The Hutterite colonies of South Dakota and Canada are further examples, considered below.

The organization of cooperating individuals into a group that recognizes a certain identity has a profound effect on the genetic composition of clans, tribes, villages, and other such political units. Within each unit, though, there are usually subunits or subpopulations that prevent homogeneous distribution of genes throughout. Studies of the Pahiro, a primitive hill tribe in the eastern part of India, have shown that the genes are not distributed evenly in this relatively small population of about 1,400. The tribe forms a breeding population and is relatively isolated from its neighbors, but it is divided into subgroups. These groups occupy neighboring villages and form—in fact—smaller breeding populations within the sociopolitical unit, the Pahiro tribe. Thus, we must be extremely cautious in any statement about gene frequency of large groups, whether nations, states, tribes or races. Reports describing the gene frequency of, say, several groups of Bantu, the Lapps, the English, or the American Indians, can be completely erroneous unless the sample is taken from representatives who are from the same breeding population within the social political unit—a difficult task but a necessary one when we attempt to understand human diversity.

The distributions of gene frequencies for certain alleles such as blood groups have been recorded for vast numbers of people. Boyd used these traits as sorting criteria in an attempt to differentiate races of mankind; the gene frequencies he reports are given in Table 4-2. These groups cover large geographical regions and include numerous breeding populations; some of them tend to describe or imply homogeneity where actually little or none exists.

Chance or "fate," natural events or intentional acts (such as of migration), play an important role in determining the growth, size, isolation, and ultimately gene frequency of the population. A typhoon may wipe out a majority of an island population, as on Puka Puka in the South Pacific, where an eighteenth-century typhoon left but seventeen survivors. These seventeen were all from the lower class in the Polynesian social structure, and Shapiro (1942) explained the shorter stature of today's population as a consequence. Starvation and disease, too, often have decimated populations, leaving only a handful to start a new generation. Descendants will often have traits or combinations of traits quite different from those expected. When studying a particular human group, the geneticist should be fully aware of its past history. Gajdusek (1964: 134) notes: "The vicissitudes of history caused by social, psychological, and natural events operating on small bands have contributed greatly to the

TABLE 4-2

Frequencies of ABO Blood Groups

(After Boyd, 1963)

Population	Place	Number Tested	O	A	B	AB
					Blood-group frequency	
American Indians:		*Low A, virtually no B*				
Toba	Argentina	194	98.5	1.5	0.0	0.0
Sioux	S. Dakota.	100	91.0	7.0	2.0	.0
		Moderate A, virtually no B				
Navaho	New Mexico	359	77.7	22.5	0.0	.0
Pueblo	New Mexico:					
	Jemez, etc.	310	78.4	20.0	1.6	.0
		High A, little B				
Bloods	Montana	69	17.4	81.2	0.0	1.4
Eskimo	Baffin Land	146	55.5	43.8	.0	0.7
Austr. Aborigines	S. Australia	54	42.6	57.4	.0	.0
Basques	San Sebastian	91	57.2	41.7	1.1	.0
American Indians:						
Shoshone	Wyoming	60	51.6	45.0	1.6	1.6
Polynesians	Hawaii	413	36.5	60.8	2.2	0.5
		Fairly high A, some B				
English	London	422	47.9	42.4	8.3	1.4
French	Paris	1,265	39.8	42.3	11.8	6.1
Armenians	From Turkey	330	27.3	53.9	12.7	6.1
Lapps	Finland	94	33.0	52.1	12.8	2.1
Melanesians	New Guinea	500	37.6	44.4	13.2	4.8
Germans	Berlin	39,174	36.5	42.5	14.5	6.5
		High A and high B				
Welsh	North Towns	192	47.9	32.8	16.2	3.1
Italians	Sicily	540	45.9	33.4	17.3	3.4
Siamese	Bangkok	213	37.1	17.8	35.2	9.9
Finns	Hame	972	34.0	42.4	17.1	6.5
Germans	Danzig	1,888	33.1	41.6	18.0	7.3
Ukrainians	Kharkov	310	36.4	38.4	21.6	3.6
Asiatic Indians	Bengal	160	32.5	20.0	39.4	8.1

determination of the evolutionary course that has led to man." To this should be added that the characteristics that set many modern human groups apart are often due to chance events or "the vicissitudes of history." Favorable location is also a big factor in population growth; witness the eightfold increase of populations of British origin over the past four centuries.

In the case of chance events mediated by certain human actions, the "Founder's Principle" (see page 41) has been a major factor in shaping the human gene pool. It certainly influences the genetic composition of future generations descended from the founding population. When *H. sapiens,* as a species, was very small in numbers during prehistoric times, the reoccurrence of the Founder's Principle would have produced much intergroup variability. The dangers of prehistoric existence probably destroyed many small groups, while of others but a few hardy and lucky souls were able to survive and reestablish the population. As long as man remained at the nomadic hunting and gathering level, a chance fluctuation in population size due to random, natural events would cause the species to remain small. There was little possibility of the formation of large homogenous breeding populations.

Several groups established in recent times have been closely studied and show some unique traits. Modern colonies of more than 10,000 Hutterites were originally established by 91 founders in 1850. The high birth rate (10.8 children per marriage) has produced an increase without new immigrants. Since gene flow into the colonies from (outside) populations is essentially zero, the Hutterites today have certain unique trait combinations.

The Amish (of Pennsylvania) started from an established 200 founders who entered Pennsylvania between 1720 and 1770; from these few a population of 45,000 was reported in 1960. This growth from a few ancestors, with little outside genetic material added, results in close inbreeding (80 percent of the families in two counties are accounted for by only eight surnames); consequently, certain recessive genetic disorders occur in high frequency (McKusick et al., 1964).

Founders or original colonists often are a select group, not a representative cross section of a parent population from which they migrated. Hulse (1957) pointed out that a great many migrants to the British colonies in North America came from certain parts of the British Isle. Also, he noted that certain physical characters were possessed by these migrants. In his study of the Italian Swiss, Hulse observed that they were generally taller and heavier than the stay-at-home group. One may suppose that such groups as the Hutterites, Dunkers, and Amish may have descended from ancestors who were not representative of the general population. These factors can result in some particular distribution of traits that sets the modern-day descendants apart. Though these factors are lumped under the term Founder's Effect or Principle, they cover a multitude of events, some chance and some intentional. The founding group also may by chance have certain recessive genes that will give rise to a high frequency of these alleles when the population expands. Livingstone (1969: 58) noted:

> . . . lethal genes are eliminated at such a slow rate in large populations. Since most of the world's populations have expanded rapidly in the last 1,000 years, much of the variability in the frequencies of

lethal genes (or non-lethals for that matter) could be a consequence of the original expansion of the major populations.

Chance and choice played a major role in establishing at least two well-known island populations. Pitcairn Islanders today are the result of interbreeding between the Bounty mutineers and a few Polynesian women from Tahiti. Chance threw them together on a remote uninhabited island, and the union of two widely different gene pools (Polynesian and British) produced a hardy, healthy group. Inhabitants of Tristan da Cunha in the South Atlantic were not quite so fortunate. From a few settlers in 1814 to 1821 the island population grew to 267 in 1962, when the island had to be evacuated because of volcanic action. Though the social structure enforced outbreeding in this group, the number of consanguineous marriages has increased. Since 1930 most islanders have married relatives, and this inbreeding has resulted in a number of congenital defects.

Once a group is established as a breeding population, the size of the reproductive unit plays an important part in determining the composition of each succeeding generation. *Genetic Drift* or *Sewall Wright Effect* refers to chance events that alter gene frequencies in small breeding populations. The effect is accentuated because even fewer individuals contribute to the next generation. In large modern populations one-fifth to one-sixth generally produce one-half of the next generation. In small, relatively isolated groups the effective breeding population is even lower, and the fact that a few males father the majority of the children can have a profound effect on the gene fixation of each generation. The Dunker Isolate in western Pennsylvania presents a good example of genetic drift. Gene frequencies for blood groups have shown significant differences between this religious isolate and the parent population in western Germany as well as the surrounding Pennsylvania populations (see Table 4-3). Glass explained these differences on the basis of the

TABLE 4-3
Dunker Isolate ABO Frequencies
(After Glass et al., 1952)

	No.	A	B	AB	O
(1) W. Germany	5,036	2,245	504	237	2,050
(Duisberg)		44.6%	10.0%	4.7%	40.7%
(2) Dunker Isolate	228	135	7	5	81
		59.3%	3.1%	2.2%	35.5%
(3) United States	30,000	11,840	3,350	1,250	13,560
(New York City		39.5%	11.2%	4.2%	45.2%
and N. Carolina)					

small size of the effective breeding population (Glass et al., 1952). This
and several more recent studies show that genetic drift is an important
factor, perhaps even the principal agent in the formation of genetic
variation among tribes, villages, and clans or any socially defined breeding
unit.

When the investigator studies groups such as the Dunkers, written
records are available to guide and aid him in establishing genealogies.
However, for nonliterate tribes such as the Amazon Indians in South
America or tribal groups in New Guinea no records exist beyond a few
notes provided by travelers, anthropologists, or missionaries, which are
not adequate to definitely establish the relationships between groups.
Therefore, identification of primitive populations is made, at least ini-
tially, on the basis of language similarities—the assumption being that
tribes who speak the same language or similar dialects of a language are
related genetically and share close common ancestry. Often the analogy
is made between the spread of language and the spread of genes, as if
the processes were the same—which they are not. As noted earlier, language is not inherited but learned. Several writers, though, have dealt
in language groups, families, dialects, and so on as if they were genetically
determined phenotypes and as if dialect marked off a breeding group.
In one study noted earlier (see page 6), Darlington claimed that there
is a parallel between frequency of type O blood and the ability to pronounce the Th sound. Peoples with a frequency of type O blood of
less than 64 percent do not have the sound in their language, while
those with greater than 64 percent do. Such correlations are not reliable,
because the ways in which gene frequency and language units change
are quite different.

Even the comparison of gene-frequency differences or similarities
between two or more populations is not a reliable means of determining
relationships or closeness of common ancestry. Though the groups may
have separated into different units only within the recent past, they
still may have quite different gene frequencies. Villages of the Xavente
Indians and groups of Yanomama, both South American Indians in the
Amazon basin, divide into groups to establish new villages when the old
settlement reaches a certain critical size. They decide who belongs to
which group on the basis of family membership, and the actual division
is usually along family lines. The effect is to produce villages whose
populations have widely divergent gene frequencies even though they
are closely related. This is the "lineal effect" described by Neel (1970:
816). If gene frequencies alone were used to establish relationship, many
erroneous conclusions would ensue.

Another case is the comparison of gene frequencies from several
villages of the islands of New Guinea. Livingstone showed significant

differences between villages in their gene frequencies, though all spoke the same language and shared common ancestry. He cautioned that blood-group frequency and language do not correlate. These genetic differences are probably due to a combination of genetic drift and Founder's Effect (Livingstone, 1963: 542). Populations on many islands of the South Pacific also have gene frequencies that are unusual in that they do not fit the expected frequency for Polynesians. Gajdusek (1964: 124) notes that on Rennell Island, with a population of 1,000, the B frequency is 57 percent, even though Polynesian populations are generally free of the type B blood-group gene. He described how raids, warfare, castaways, and other events can rapidly change the genetic structure of a population. The introduction of captives, especially females, as slaves into the community can have a dramatic effect on the population's composition. Chagnon and associates reported that a Makiritare woman brought into a Yanomama village as a captive was responsible for introducing the Diego gene. The frequency of the gene increased within two generations and became higher in the Yanomama than in the Makiritare village from which the captive came.

Another interesting example of the Founder's Principle is porphyria in South African populations. The gene that causes this metabolic defect (failure to metabolize the porphyrin ring properly) was introduced by a young girl from Rotterdam. She married another recent immigrant from Holland in 1688, and the 8,000 carriers of this gene can be traced to their marriage.

Polygamy may have been the preferred form of marriage in former times, and it can be an important factor in producing the next generation. In some modern groups where this form of marriage is practiced 70 to 80 percent of the offspring issue from polygamous unions. Since some males are able to acquire more than one wife, it is obvious that many other males have limited opportunity to reproduce; hence the genetic contribution to succeeding generations is limited to a very few males. Some males, because of their dominant position as clan leaders or relatives of high-status individuals, are going to contribute disproportionately to future generations. This reduces gene flow and acts much like the Founder's Principle in producing a certain gene combination. Polygamy may have been an important force in man's evolution, especially during periods when the strongest, bravest, or best hunter was able to acquire more wives. The Eskimo, for example, have been very practical in caring for widows and orphans. The survivors of a recently deceased hunter of the band are moved into the household of the most successful hunter, whose duty it is to care for them, taking the widow as his second or third wife and the children as his own.

If a breeding population is viewed as a unit that contains a portion

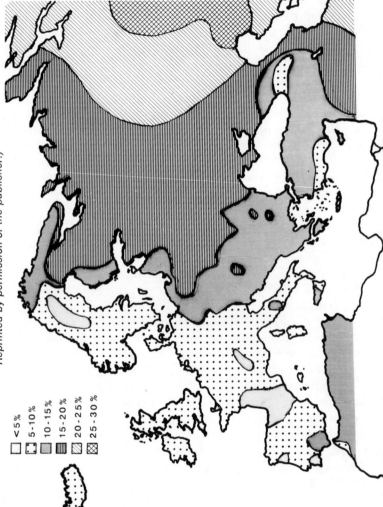

FIGURE 4-2

Frequencies of B Allele in Europe

(Copyright © 1954 by Blackwell Scientific Publications, Ltd. Reprinted by permission of the publisher.)

Legend:
- <5 %
- 5 - 10 %
- 10 - 15 %
- 15 - 20 %
- 20 - 25 %
- 25 - 30 %

of the total genome of the species, then a city, town, village, or even tribe is not necessarily a breeding unit. A breeding population is the most narrowly restricted group of individuals that interbreed a majority of the time. The Parma Valley (Italy), the Pahara (India), and Amazon villages all show that within any sociopolitical unit there may be smaller subgroupings with restricted mating circles that make up the actual breeding population. The genetic diversity between groups then may be an artifact of the socially established boundaries, and these boundaries cause the clustering of genes in both time and space.

CLINAL DISTRIBUTION OF TRAITS

It is clear that our primary objective—to understand the origin and significance of polymorphic variability—still eludes us. (Neel, 1970: 819)

We consider now the final concept of human trait distribution. The concept of *clinal distribution* or *clinal variation* traces the geographical range of phenotypic or genetic characteristics of our species and assumes that they are distributed in a meaningful way. Clines locate a trait, gene, or characteristic on a map much as barometric pressure or temperature is plotted on a weather map; they express traits that vary continuously in space, or gradual progressions of some feature from one geographical region to the next. The variation of skin color among the world's population is an example (see Figure 1-9). On this map the density of melanin content of the skin shows a correlation with latitude; the further north one traces the distribution, the lighter the skin pigmentation. In Figure 4-2 a distribution for the blood-group-B gene is traced throughout Europe.

These distributions pass through many populations as if they were entirely independent of the boundaries constructed by man's mating habits. However, the spatial location of the populations causes the formation of a gradual series of genetic or phenotypic frequencies. The construction of a line through these forms the *cline*. The fact that the location of populations forms the cline makes it very difficult to explain the distribution of a single gene, though several workers have advocated such an approach. Livingston (1964: 54) claims: "The variability in the frequency of any gene can be plotted in the same way that temperature is plotted on a weather map."

Figure 4-3 shows how within any single area, as the distribution is better understood, broad clinal expressions break down. Compare this with Figure 4-2.

FIGURE 4-3

Distributions of B Allele in France and Italy

(Adapted from Morganti, 1959; Vallois and Marquer, 1964.)

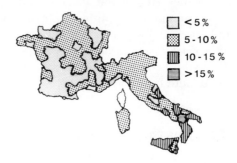

☐ < 5 %

▨ 5 - 10 %

▥ 10 - 15 %

▤ > 15 %

There are several possible explanations for clinical distributions. The one most frequently offered is that clines indicate the effect of natural selection. This means that gene frequency follows distribution of selective forces, but clines can also indicate an exchange or flow of genes between populations. It has been suggested that clines may be due to recent advances of advantageous genes or to gene flow between populations with different equilibrium frequencies for the gene (Livingstone, 1964). Figure 4-4 shows the geographical distribution of hemoglobin S gene in the Old World superimposed upon a map of the distribution of Falciparum Malaria. The gene appears to provide a selective advantage in a malarial environment, as will be explained in the next chapter. Note should be made of the fact that Hb[s] is not confined to Africa but occurs in many other areas and in numerous diverse populations.

Notice, finally, that a vast majority of human genes are shared by all populations. Only the frequency of occurrence of these alleles in adjacent populations differs—and these differences provide us with the clines.

BREEDING POPULATIONS VS. CLINES

It has often been assumed that subspecific groupings based on the distribution of one, or at most a few characters, will necessarily be concordant with the distributions of other variable characters. This, it seems, may be so for populations isolated in mountains, islands, caves or other restricted and special habitats, but is not usually the case in wider, more continuous regions. (Barnicot, 1964: 198)

Here is one of the major objections to the use of populations as units of study. Some feel that the proper method for studying human variability

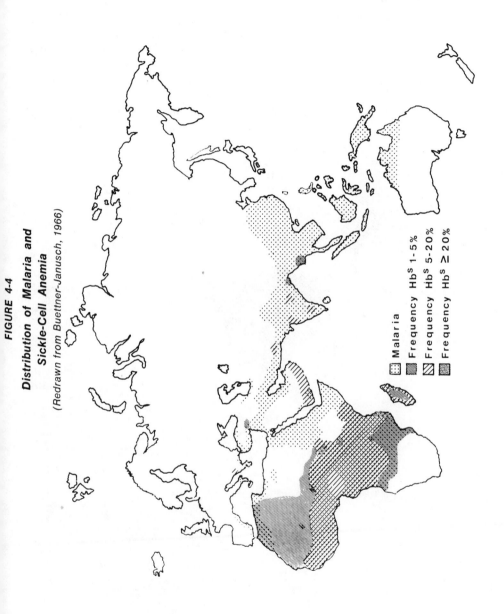

FIGURE 4-4

Distribution of Malaria and Sickle-Cell Anemia

(Redrawn from Buettner-Janusch, 1966)

Malaria

Frequency Hb^S 1-5%

Frequency Hb^S 5-20%

Frequency Hb^S ≥ 20%

111

is the single trait, as it is distributed across population boundaries. What we should be concerned with is not taxonomic units but with the distribution of traits among the world's peoples and the meaning of this variation.

A portion of this variation is illustrated by the maps in Figures 1-9, 4-3 and 4-5. These coincide with the distribution of certain selective

FIGURE 4-5

The Distribution of Stature of Male Indians
(Adapted from Newman, 1953)

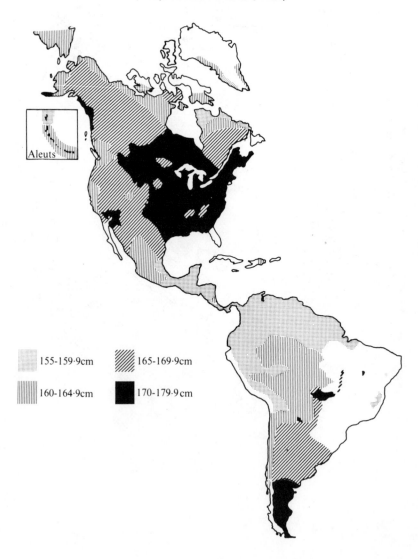

155-159·9cm   165-169·9cm

160-164·9cm   170-179·9 cm

forces and, in several striking examples, also with massive population movements. The presence of a darkly pigmented cline in North America and the presence of Hb^s is due to movements of large numbers of Africans to the New World during the seventeenth and eighteenth centuries. This illustrates why modern populations may not provide evidence of evolutionary history. However, the distribution of Rh— (cde) in Europe, and North Africa may indicate prior contact between groups living in these areas (the occupation of Spain and parts of Southern Europe by North Africans during the seventh and eighth centuries).

The distribution of body forms shown in Figure 4-5 follows climatic conditions closely, with the smaller persons living in tropical regions. This suggests that small body size is favored in certain environments, and those populations with the longest history of living under such conditions have been selected for their survival efficiency. This distribution ignores groups that have arrived in the recent past (Europeans).

The clines illustrated in the figures describe the distribution of both monogenic and polygenic traits, and there are, as previously discussed, major distinctions between them. Morphological phenotypes such as skin color or body size vary continuously, and each population or group grades imperceptibly into another, no sharp clear-cut divisions being discernible. This forms a smooth clinal distribution. In the case of monogenetic traits, gene frequencies within a population are used to establish a cline; we have seen that these frequencies can change rapidly in a single generation. A simple comparison between trait distributions and selective forces, then, is not always possible.

If we take account of those factors that cause changes in gene frequency—mutation, natural selection, genetic drift, migration and breeding behavior—then we find that factors 1 and 2 act on certain alleles in unique ways. Factor 2, natural selection, is determined by environmental conditions and is distributed geographically; and of course it cuts across population boundaries (which are culturally established). The other factors, however, have a strong influence on gene frequency, but they are behaviorally determined (as described in the previous section) and they have an intense effect on the gene frequency from generation to generation. Genes are not passed on one at a time, nor is individual fitness determined by single genes. An individual's genes are transmitted as a group, and fitness is a compromise between the interaction of all of the genes. Lewontin (1970: 44) has described the situation:

> The important genetic discovery of Thomas Hunt Morgan and Calvin Bridges, something which population genetics in general does not take into account, is that genes are not floating around as individual particles. If you make a theory of population genetics that

includes the fact that genes are organized on chromosomes, then you get the curious result that no single locus can be shown to have any important natural selection, that the chromosome will evolve as a kind of block by the accumulation of very small effects, and that natural selection may be operating to stabilize the frequency of the genes within a population. But one will not find that out by examining the effect of a simple locus substitution at a single locus. One has to take into account the entire chromosomal array.

Gene flow is often described as a major cause of clinal variation, but it is not descriptive of actual events, because genes do not flow or "float around in space." They are transmitted as a group or an array by the chromosomes, and the way these groups are combined to produce the next generation is determined by society. These factors lend considerable support to the breeding population concept. Hiernaux (1964: 32) remarks:

> To me, as to many others, it seems that the only useful way of grouping individuals for anthropological analysis is to group together the people participating within the same circle of matings.

The clinal approach has its strength, but only when used in conjunction with the actual basis for trait distribution—the population. The argument that one is more efficient as a means of studying human variation than the other is without foundation. We must consider both in order to understand man's diversity. In the next chapter we shall consider the adaptive significance or survival value of this diversity.

RECOMMENDED READINGS AND
LITERATURE CITED

ABBIE, ANDREW. 1963. "Comments: *Geographic and Microgeographic Races,* by Marshall T. Newman (189–192)," *Current Anthrop.,* 4: 192–193.

BAKER, PAUL T. 1967. "The biological race concept as a research tool," *Am. J. Phys. Anthrop.,* 27: 21–25.

BARNICOT, NIGEL A. 1964. "Taxonomy and variation in modern man," in *The Concept of Race,* Ashley Montagu, ed. New York: The Free Press, pp. 180–227.

BOYD, WM. C. 1963. "Genetics and the human race," *Science,* 140: 1057–1064.

BRIERLEY, J. K. 1970. *A Natural History of Man.* Cranbury, N.J.: Fairleigh Dickinson University Press.

CHAGNON, NAPOLEON A., JAMES V. NEEL, LOWELL WEITKAMP, HENRY GERSHOWITZ, and MANUEL AYRES. 1970. "The influence of cultural factors on the demography and pattern of gene flow from the Makiritare to the Yanomama Indians," *Am. J. Phys. Anthrop.,* 32: 339–350.

DARLINGTON, C. D. 1947. "The genetic component of language," *Heredity*, 1: 269–286.

DOBZHANSKY, THEODOSIUS. 1944. "On species and races of living and fossil man," *Am. J. Phys. Anthrop.*, 2: 251–255.

EHRLICH, P. R. and R. W. HOLM. 1962. "Patterns and populations," *Science*, 137: 652–657.

EHRLICH, PAUL R. and PETER H. RAVEN. 1969. "Differentiation of populations," *Science*, 165: 1228–1232.

GAJDUSEK, D. CARLETON. 1964. "Factors governing the genetics of primitive human populations," *Cold Spring Harbor Symposia in Quantitative Biology*, 29: 121–135.

GARN, STANLEY M. 1961. *Human Races*. Springfield, Ill.: Charles C Thomas.

GILES, EUGENE. 1962. "Favism, sex-linkage, and the Indo-European kinship system," *Southwest J. Anthrop.*, 18(3): 286–290.

GLASS, BENTLEY, MILTON S. SACKS, ELSA F. JAHN, and CHARLES HESS. 1952. "Genetic drift in a religious isolate; an analysis of the causes of variation in blood group and other gene frequencies in a small population," *The American Naturalist*, 86: 145–159.

HIERNAUX, JEAN. 1964. "The concept of race and the taxonomy of mankind," in *The Concept of Race*, Ashley Montagu, ed. New York: The Free Press, pp. 29–45.

———. 1966. "Human biological diversity in Central Africa," *Man*, 1(3): 287–306.

———. 1971. "Ethnic differences in growth and development," in *The Biological and Social Meaning of Race*, Richard H. Osborne, ed. San Francisco: W. H. Freeman & Co., pp. 39–55.

HOOTON, EARNEST A. 1936. "Plain statements about race," *Science*, 83: 511–513.

HULSE, FREDERICK S. 1957. "Some factors influencing the relative proportions of human racial stocks," *Cold Spring Harbor Symposia in Quantitative Biology*, 22: 33–45.

LEWONTIN, RICHARD. 1970. "The nature of human variation," *Engineering and Science* 33(6): 44.

LIVINGSTONE, FRANK B. 1963. "Blood groups and ancestry: A test case from the New Guinea highlands," *Current Anthrop.*, 4: 541–542.

———. 1964. "On the nonexistence of human races," in *The Concept of Race*, Ashley Montagu, ed. New York: The Free Press, pp. 46–60.

———. 1969. "The founder effect and deleterious genes," *Am. J. Phys. Anthrop.*, 30: 55–60.

MCKUSICK, VICTOR A., JOHN A. HOSTETLER, JANICE A. EGELAND, and ROSWELL ELDRIDGE. 1964. "The distribution of certain genes in the Old Order Amish," *Cold Spring Harbor Symposia in Quantitative Biology*, 29: 99–114.

MAYR, ERNST. 1963. *Animal Species and Evolution*. Cambridge, Mass.: The Belknap Press of Harvard University.

MORGANTI, G. 1959. "Distributions of blood groups in Italy," in *Medical Biology and Etruscan Origins*, G. E. W. Wolstenholme and C. M. O'Connor, eds. Ciba Foundation Symposium, Churchill, London. Boston: Little, Brown and Company.

NEEL, JAMES V. 1970. "Lessons from a 'primitive' people," *Science*, 170: 815–822.

NEWMAN, MARSHALL. 1953. "The application of ecological rules to the racial anthropology of the aboriginal New World," *Am. Anthrop.*, 55(1): 311–327.

SHAPIRO, H. L. 1942. "The anthropometry of Puka Puka," *Anthrop. Papers Mus. Nat. His.*, 38: 141–169.

SLOTKIN, J. S. 1965. *Readings in Early Anthropology.* Viking Fund Publications in Anthropology, no. 40.

VALLOIS, H. V. and P. MARQUER. 1964. "La Répartition en France des Groupes Sanguins ABO," *BMSA,* vol. 6, 9th Series, no. 1, pp. 1–200.

chapter five

The Adaptive Significance of Man's Variation

An all too often forgotten and yet most basic fact is that the genes do not determine traits or characters, but rather the ways in which the organism responds to the environment. (Dobzhansky, 1971: 121)

Within each ecological framework created by the interactions between a group of organisms and the environment there is a certain potential for survival. The behavior of each individual of the group, as well as his total genome, endows him with a certain capacity to live and to reproduce, and through reproduction a part of this capacity is passed on to the next generation. This *survival potential* is an important factor in evolution. In this chapter we will discuss the survival potential determined by the interrelationships between man's behavior (culture), the environment, and the genetic diversity of certain populations.

We assume that gene combinations for several well-known characteristics are adaptively significant; that is, natural selection has acted over a period of time to form the gene pool of the populations so it is composed of a majority of individuals best suited to the environment. The genotypes and the resulting phenotypes enable the individual to respond efficiently to environmental stresses. However, man's complex behavior and his often elaborate technology interfere with and modify these stresses. The wearing of clothing, use of artificial shelter, cooking of food, use of domesticated plants and animals, medication, sanitation, and so on, all have had their effects on the modification of environmental stresses and have actually created what can truly be called man's environment. But man's skill in manipulating the environment should not be looked upon as a means of totally freeing him from the effects of natural selection. The environment, or man's environment, still exerts stress on human populations and exacts a toll; natural selection still functions to influence gene-pool composition. The technology changes the intensity of selection or alters it completely.

Many types of stresses or environmental factors act upon man. These are too numerous to list individually, and many have effects on the metabolism that are not altogether understood. For our present purposes we will consider the following as environmental stresses that have important effects on human diversity and probably have significant influence on man's evolution: (1) temperature and humidity, (2) solar radiation, (3) altitude, (4) nutrition, (5) disease. Unfortunately, none of these has a simple causal relationship with man's genetic system, and a single stress may effect several genotypes. Body form is related to several factors, particularly diet and climate; also, the polygenic makeup that influences growth and form of the individual provides him with a certain potential response to these factors. Other polygenic characteristics are equally complex. We will attempt to show here some of the probable relationships of the genotypes and phenotypes discussed in Chapter 3 as varying widely between human populations; skin color will be the first one we will consider.

SKIN COLOR, GEOGRAPHY, AND NATURAL SELECTION

The distribution of deeply pigmented peoples of the world, as noted earlier, shows the darkest skinned to be the inhabitants of a world zone roughly defined by the Tropics of Cancer and of Capricorn (see Figure 1-9). Within this zone there is the most intense solar radiation throughout the year. Total solar radiation varies little in relationship to latitude, while that of the shorter wavelengths of the spectrum (in the ultraviolet 290-mμ to 320-mμ range) changes rapidly with an increase in latitude. It is this part of the solar radiation spectrum that causes sunburn and sun tanning and stimulates the synthesis of vitamin D_3 from 7-dehydrocholesterol.[1] Seasonal changes cause wide variation in the amount of ultraviolet light reaching the earth's surface in the temperate zones. At, or near, the

---

[1] For further discussion see Loomis, 1967 and 1970, also Blum, 1969.

equator there is much less variation in solar intensity in the ultraviolet region of 290 to 320 mμ.

The distribution of dark-skinned peoples coincident with solar radiation has caused writers for many years to argue that skin color has adaptive significance and that in some way these people are suited for the climatic conditions under which they live. Such an argument often was countered by observations that several of these populations lived in humid tropical rainforest where little sunlight reached the ground and, in fact, these tropical peoples had the darkest skins. Further, such conditions would have prevented solar radiation in these regions from becoming an effective selective force. Both arguments frequently have been based on scant evidence of degree of pigmentation and a considerable misunderstanding of several significant factors: the nature of solar radiation, its effect on the skin, simple physical geography, and the living conditions of many tropical peoples. Discussions of human pigmentation are, in fact, often purely speculative with little reference to the available data. We will try to take up the factors one at a time and to consider whether the melanin content of the human skin is, in fact, advantageous or disadvantageous under certain environmental conditions.

Solar Radiation

Figure 5-1 illustrates the spectrum of solar radiation and the intensity of various portions. The absorption bands provide a rough approximation of the effective interference that certain substances will provide. The *visible portion,* 400 to 800 mμ (4000–8000 angstroms), is least affected by atmospheric conditions, while water vapor is especially influential in reducing the amounts of infrared striking the earth's surface. Infrared is the part of the spectrum that causes a rise in skin temperature and provides the warm feeling one gets while in the sunlight. The *ultraviolet* portion, about 290 to 320 mμ is absorbed by ozone but is relatively unaffected by water vapor, a factor which explains why one can become sunburned even on an overcast summer day. The energy is affected also by time of day, as shown in Figure 5-2 (part A). Curve 1 shows the intensity of the sun at zenith and curve 2 at four hours from zenith, at a time when the ultraviolet is almost zero (refer to part of curve below 4000 angstroms).

Human Skin and Solar Radiation

The effects of solar energy on the skin vary considerably depending on wavelength (Figure 5-2, part C); penetration of the skin is deepest at the near infrared, while very little ultraviolet enters the lower layer of the

FIGURE 5-1

Measure of Energy of Solar Radiation Reaching the Earth Relative to Energy Dissipated in Atmosphere

(After Luckeish, 1948, and Coon, 1965)

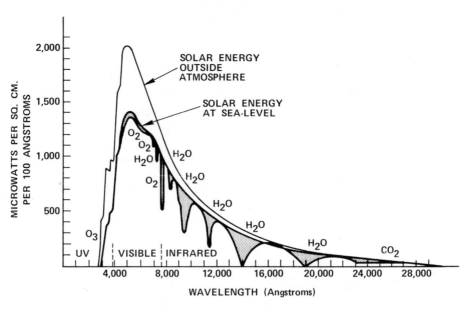

Absorption Bands of CO_2, H_2O, O_2 and O_3

epidermis (stratum germinativum). More darkly pigmented skin is penetrated much less than fair skin, as shown by the W and N curves. These

FIGURE 5-2 *(See facing page)*

A. Spectral Distribution of Sunlight at the Surface of the Earth (after Moon, 1941). Curve 1, with sun at zenith. Curve 2, with sun at 60° (four hours) from zenith. V, spectral limits of human vision. E, spectral limits (within sunlight) for sunburn, antirachitic action and cancer induction.

B. Diagrammatic Representation of Skin Structures. A schematized conception in which the dimensions should not be taken as generally representative, since the skin may vary widely in its thickness. c, corneum, i.e., horny layer of epidermis. m, malpighian layer of epidermis. sw., sweat gland. seb., sebaceous gland. p, the most superficial blood vessels, arterioles, capillaries, and venules. h, hair follicle. s, hair shaft.

C. Penetration of Light into Human Skin as a Function of Wavelength. The curves N and W indicate for Negro and White skin, respectively, *rough estimates* of depths at which radiation of the corresponding wavelengths is reduced to 5 percent of its incident value. There are insufficient data to make more than rough estimates, and these curves should be regarded as suggestive rather than in any way exact (see text). Curve W is based on Hardy and Muschenheim (1934, 1936), and on Kirby-Smith, Blum, and Grady (1942). Curve N is based on Hardy and Muschenheim (1934, 1936) and on Thompson (1955).

differences may be important factors in adaptation to incidence of high solar radiation, as will be shown below. The final part of Figure 5-2 illustrates some of the principal structures found in the dermis.

FIGURE 5-2

Solar Energy and Skin Structure

(Redrawn from Blum, 1962)

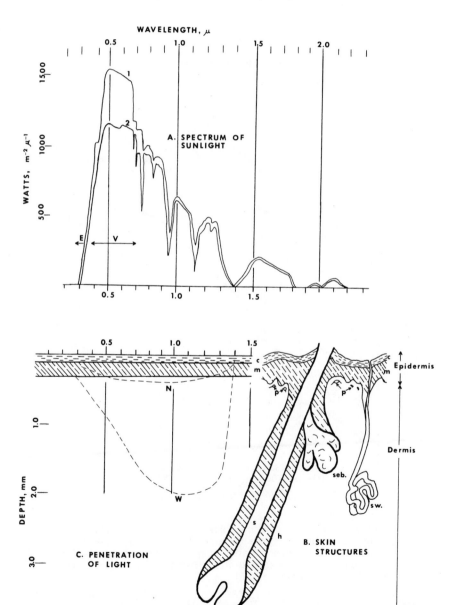

Since we judge skin color by the visible part of the spectrum, the differences in the reflective properties of human skin should be noted. Figure 5-3 shows skin-reflectance characteristics of American Negroes and American whites. The curves indicate greater reflectance by the white skin over the entire spectral range tested. These curves, however, were constructed from average values of all subjects tested and probably obscure range of variation of reflectance. Figure 5-4 illustrates the range of reflectance characteristics of several populations who have varying degrees

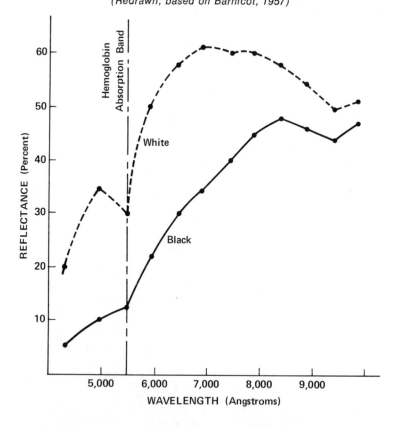

FIGURE 5-3

Skin Reflectance Characteristics of a Sample of American Blacks and Whites

(Redrawn; based on Barnicot, 1957)

Average reflectance characteristics of Negro and white skin on the flexor surface of the forearm. Measurements made from visible light to the near infrared range with marked absorption indicated in the white sample at approximately 5500 angstroms (the absorption for hemoglobin).

of pigmentation. Reflectance was measured at the upper end of the visible range. The whites reflected roughly 50 percent of the light while Aborigines only reflected about 10 percent; other groups showed reflectance

FIGURE 5-4

Skin-Reflectance Characteristics of Several Populations
(After Walsh, 1963)

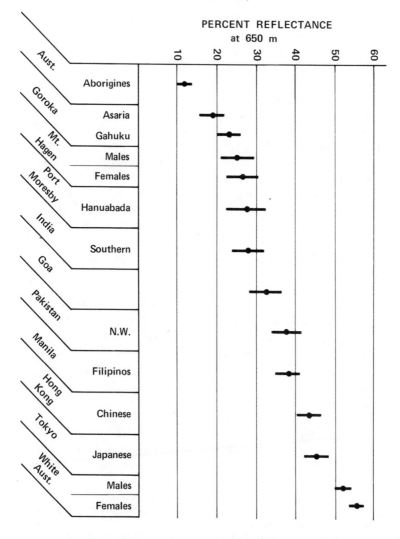

The mean percentage of reflectance from the foreheads of samples of several populations is indicated by the dot, and the range of plus or minus one standard deviation is indicated by the line.

properties between these two extremes. The two groups which recorded male and female reflectance values showed males lower on the scale.

As we sum up these factors we should keep in mind the following; first, the incidence of ultraviolet in the tropics is least affected by seasonal changes, but ultraviolet has low skin penetrating power. Further, water vapor does not reduce this part of the spectrum. Second, reflectance properties of skin are such that visible light is reflected more by lighter skin than by dark, but the infrared penetrates more deeply in fair skin. This would mean that darker-skinned peoples would have a lower threshold of warmth, as several experiments have shown, but fairer skin would benefit more from the warming effects of the infrared rays, owing to their degree of penetration.

A word about geography and the living habits of tropical peoples is appropriate here. With the few exceptions of wandering, hunting, and gathering peoples who dwell in tropical rainforest as refuge areas, most populations who live in tropical areas sustain themselves by agriculture or herding. Agriculturists must remove forest and hence protective shade covering; pastoral herding peoples must live in open country. The argument that many darker-skinned peoples live in shaded areas of the tropical rainforests is incorrect. The fact is that a good many of these peoples live under conditions of a high incidence of solar radiation, especially that portion that is responsible for sun tanning, sunburn, and vitamin D synthesis. The few exceptions in the Old and New World tropics are explainable in terms of the population's history, as will be discussed below.

Northward from the equator populations become fairer skinned, and this factor supports the argument for relationships between skin and sun. We can now consider some of the probable explanations for these distributions. First, if we look upon the epidermis as a filter which reduces the amount of solar radiation penetrating the skin, we can establish an advantage for high melanin content of the skin. Dark-skinned peoples are less prone to sunburn; thus there is a reduction in the detrimental effects of overexposure to solar radiation.[2]

Of course, man can and often does use some kind of shelter or covering for his body, but in certain climates this is a disadvantage and is often detrimental to the body's capacity for heat dissipation. Skin pigmentation enables man to be more mobile and functional in tropical sunlight, where

---

[2] Sunburn, depending on the degree, can cause erythema (congestion of the subcutaneous capillaries), destruction of certain cells, and edema or collection of fluids under the skin's surface. Besides being painful it can in the extreme be very dangerous, opening the way for many secondary effects including infection, heat exhaustion, and so on.

ambient temperatures are close to man's normal body temperatures, making metabolic heat dissipation difficult.

Another factor of excessive exposure to solar radiation is the development of skin cancer. The filtering effect of the skin apparently reduces the incidence of skin cancer, which rarely ever occurs in deeply pigmented people. However, this is a rare disease even in the fair-skinned (approximately 1 in 1,000 persons) and usually is of late onset—towards the end of a person's reproductive period. As a consequence it should have had little effect on natural selection.

As explained earlier, vitamin D (or, more correctly, calciferol) is essential for proper calcium metabolism. This vitamin is synthesized by action of ultraviolet light on a sterol compound, 7-dehydrocholesterol, in the lower layers of the epidermis, probably in the granular layer (see Loomis, 1970). Since the amount required for proper maintenance of calcium is small, about 400 units per day, the exposure of a small area of the body to the sun for a short period is sufficient. It has been estimated that 20 square centimeters, or about the area of the skin covering a human infant's face, is sufficient. Any interference with this exposure—reduction in time, reduction in amount of ultraviolet or surface area—will correspondingly diminish the amount of vitamin D synthesized. The effects of this reduction in the vitamin vary between individuals, depending on age. Infants and children in pre-adolescence, the period of rapid growth of the skeleton, will suffer most severely, sometimes even fatally, as reported often in European populations during the nineteenth century. In adults, vitamin D deficiency prevents mineralization of newly formed bone matrix. In extreme cases this results in softened bones which are subject to distortion and which fracture more easily.[3]

The importance of sunlight is further documented by evidence from certain societies that seclude their women throughout most of their lives. Infants in Moslem cultures and among high-caste Hindus often contact rickets during infancy, but many recover as young children when they are allowed to play out of doors. Females, often married at 12 years of age and then forced into seclusion, frequently develop the disease again. Rickets and osteomalacia in females are effective as selective forces in the population because any distortion of the pelvic region is apt to reduce a woman's chances of giving normal birth. A reduction in the number of live children she will produce is likely, and a shortening of her own life-span is possible because of an increased chance of death during delivery.

---

[3] Osteomalacia and osteoporosis in adults appears to be a major problem throughout our species. Both conditions result in poorly mineralized bone, but the causes are complex and somewhat different. Osteomalacia is basically the failure of newly formed bone to mineralize and is due to a deficiency in vitamin D or phosphorus.

Since darkly pigmented people synthesize less calciferol, pigmentation is a handicap in northern latitudes to people of darkly pigmented skin. In fact, rickets was rampant among Negro children living in northern United States cities half a century ago. Since then, the addition of vitamin D to milk in the United States and most European countries has all but eliminated this childhood disease. In the tropics deeply pigmented skin can be an advantage, since it prevents the overproduction of vitamin D, which is just as detrimental as too little of the vitamin.[4]

Skin Color and Evolution

Considering all these factors that relate skeletal structure, calcium metabolism, skin pigmentation, and incidence of ultraviolet radiation, we now ask: How have they affected man's evolution? Is *H. sapiens'* color "naturally dark"—and, if so, what accounts for the depigmentation of the Europeans? The wealth of fossil evidence accumulating today supports earlier contentions that man evolved in the tropics.

Our immediate ancestors spread into and "permanently" occupied the northern latitudes relatively recently in time, probably not before the third interglacial period. At this time these prehistoric men (Neanderthal) were likely dark skinned and suffered the detrimental effects common to deeply pigmented peoples living in regions of low ultraviolet radiation. Many skeletal lesions found among fossilized Neanderthal remains suggest that they had suffered from rickets.[5]

Selection for peoples that could thrive under such climatic conditions —that is, depigmented or fair-skinned peoples—has lasted until the present century, and there is evidence that the adjustment to new selective forces must have taken many thousands of years. Even during the Mesolithic period, a time between 10,000 and 15,000 years ago, Northern European populations must have suffered from poor mineralization. Skeletal remains from Sweden dating to this period show many signs of poor calcium metabolism in their teeth and bones.

Two things made possible the continuous survival of man in the northern latitudes. The first is the steady decline in pigmentation through-

---

[4] Whole-body radiation has been estimated to produce upwards of 120,000 units of calciferol per hour, which is well above the toxic level (between 10,000 and 100,000 units per day). Clothing, of course, will reduce the amount of skin exposed, but the reader should remember the relatively little use of clothing by tropical peoples. Besides, children the first few years seldom wear any clothing at all and during the day are much more active than adults, which would add to the degree of their exposure and hence the potential for producing toxic levels of vitamin D.

[5] Francis Ivanhoe (1970) discussed the probability that Neanderthals during the final glaciation (Wurm) suffered from vitamin D deficiency. He claims that there are numerous skeletal lesions similar to the type caused by vitamin D deficiency.

out the generations—or, rather, selection favoring the survival of individuals whose genetic systems cause them to have lighter skins. The second is the increased use of fish, particularly herring, and hence of fish oils in the diet, probably during the last 6,000 years. Eventually, though no one knows where the custom began, a home remedy for rickets was introduced—the use of fish liver oils. Also there developed the practice of placing infants outside, even during the coldest winter months, to gain a little "fresh air and sunshine." Both of these measures have the same end results and have enabled man to sustain life and maintain large populations in Northern Europe.

These examples of skin color depigmentation and certain facets of man's behavior illustrate the adaptive significance of melanin variation. Light skin has a survival value in the north and dark skin is favored in the tropics. If another feature of human skin is considered, its tanning ability, then evidence can be added to that discussed above. Selection appears to have been for skin that will vary in pigmentation according to the incidence of ultraviolet. The best adapted then would have skin that tanned well in the summer (reducing vitamin D synthesis as exposure to sunlight increased with the long summer days) and lightened during the winter to take all possible advantage of the weak winter sun. Europeans native to Southern Europe, North Africans, and Western Asian populations have skins with a higher degree of melanin content than their northern neighbors, so they tan much better—a feature which is a significant advantage in their climates.[6]

Skin coloration happens to be much more complex and variable than is usually appreciated and it requires far more discussion than can be given it here, but many of the interrelationships seem clearly established between sunlight and man's physiology. One final consideration we should notice is the difference between the skin color of males and females in the same populations. The females have lighter skin, which, given their need for a more carefully regulated calcium metabolism, makes good adaptive sense. Children also are much fairer than their parents; often the infants of dark-skinned parents are pink, and their skin steadily darkens throughout childhood. This is another factor that shows the interrelationship between the human skin-pigmentation system and solar radiation, demonstrating again the selective advantages that variable skin pigmentation can confer upon the human population.

[6] The populations that prove to be exceptions to this general distribution scheme, Northern Asians and American Indians, have a different history than Northern Europeans. American and Siberian populations, for example, probably have not lived for very long in the regions where they are found now, and natural selection for light skin has not operated for the length of time that it has in Europeans.

ABNORMAL HEMOGLOBINS
AND RED-CELL VARIANTS

The geographic distribution of the major red-cell variants and hemoglobins conforms very well to the distribution of the incidence of malaria infection. Populations with a long history of contact with the disease usually exhibit the highest frequency of red-cell deficiencies or hemoglobin abnormalities which were described earlier. These distributions are shown in Figure 4-5, and the apparent relationships between the gene frequency of certain abnormalities in a population are explained on the basis of a hypothesis that states: an individual who is a heterozygote or carrier of the abnormal gene enjoys a certain degree of immunity to infection by the malarial parasite. This would result in a reduced number of parasites in the bloodstream, hence a longer, healthier lifespan, less infant mortality, and a higher rate of fertility. For example, in the case of the sickle-cell gene Hb^s, the heterozygote Hb^aHb^s would be at a selective advantage and reproduce at a higher rate than the normal Hb^aHb^a, which would maintain the gene Hb^s at a high frequency in the population despite the loss of the gene through the near lethal combination in the homozygote Hb^sHb^s (a person homozygous for Hb^s seldom reaches adulthood).

Malaria and Natural Selection

The dread disease malaria occurs in endemic proportions in many areas of the world, mainly tropical and subtropical regions. It is a major cause of death, accounting for about four million deaths annually. If deaths due to complications arising from malarial infection (mostly nephritis) are counted, then the death rate is much higher. In areas of the world where the death rate from all causes is extremely high, recent control of malaria has reduced this rate by one third to one half. This event shows the rather stringent control that malaria exerts on population size; it probably has been a major selective force acting on mankind for many generations. The negative effects of malaria, however, are seen in many other ways besides death rates. The chronic malarial conditions that exist among tropical populations cause a lowering of the general health of the population, reduce energy levels of the people, and increase disease susceptibility, all of which is going to affect the overall fertility rates (see Livingstone, 1958 and 1971).

The interrelationships between man, his behavior, and his environment are most clearly seen in the example of malaria. This disease is caused by a protozoan parasite that spends part of its life cycle in man and part in certain species of mosquito. The organism is transmitted to man by the bite of a mosquito, or the insect may pick up the organism from biting an infected person and then become a carrier or vector which can deposit the organism in an uninfected person.

The part man plays in this host-vector disease organism scheme is important and complicated, since several of the major species of mosquito depend on human disruption of the environment to provide breeding places. The *Anopheles gambiae* mosquito, a major vector for the most virulent form of malaria, falciparum, is best suited for living around human habitations, since it does not breed well in virgin tropical rainforest; also, sedentary human populations provide many hosts. In the past these insects or their ancestral forms may have preyed upon non-human hosts, as many species still do, but through the development of sedentary life since the Neolithic several mosquitos have come to depend upon man as their major host. Man's primitive agricultural activities and his adoption of sedentary village life have brought about many changes in the environment, which have been followed by a significant increase in population compared to the nomadic hunting and gathering phase.

The slash-and-burn techniques of the tropical rainforest horticulturist drives away many mammals, which might have been the prior hosts to the mosquitos. The removal of the tropical rainforest cover exposes the thin soils to erosion, and stagnant water provides breeding places for mosquitos; further, man builds his dwellings where numerous families live in close contact. All of these events provide an ideal situation for the transmission of malarial parasites on a continuous basis, causing 100 percent of the population to be infected with them.

It is believed that these relationships have existed for as long as man has practiced agriculture in the tropics—about six thousand years. The situation in the subtropics is more complex, and the vectors are different as well as the types of malarial disease that they cause. But the association between agriculture, settled village life, and malaria is probably the same. Skeletal remains from Greek Neolithic sites show extensive signs of bone modification associated with chronic anemia, and some investigators believe these conditions to be due to thalassemia, which today is found in many Mediterranean populations suffering from malaria (see Angel, 1966).

If the malarial hypothesis is accepted, then the genes for such abnormalities as Hb^s, Hb^e, thalassemia, and G6PD deficiency are an advantage for populations living in the areas where malaria is endemic. The survival value of being a carrier living under malarious conditions is much greater than that of the normal homozygote and outweighs any detriment associated with possessing a single abnormal gene. However, as is happening today, once malaria is removed as a menace, as in our own country, the person who possesses two normal genes will be better adapted than the carrier because of the increased oxygen-carrying capacity. What mechanism actually conveys the advantage under conditions of malarial infection is not actually known, but several preliminary studies have produced results which suggest that heterozygous red cells are less able to support the malarial parasite, so there is less opportunity for the parasites to increase their number in a person who is a heterozygote for the red-cell abnormalities.

The most clear-cut relationship between malaria and the red-cell variants appears in the case of the sickle-cell hemoglobin Hb^s. Individuals who are sicklers (heterozygotes) are less likely to die from falciparum malaria than persons with normal hemoglobin; also, fertility is higher among sicklers living in areas where falciparum malaria is endemic, and female sicklers have a higher live birth rate than nonsicklers. Overall there is a significantly greater number of sicklers in the over-45 segments of the population, which indicates a longer lifespan; in addition, fewer sicklers die in infancy. Male fertility is likely to be higher in sicklers because of fewer episodes of the high fever associated with malarial attacks. Since spermatogenesis is impaired by elevated body temperature, it is believed that sicklers are less subject to this impairment to fertility, since they will have fewer malarial attacks.

Because of the concordant distribution of malaria and red-cell variants, we assume that persons who have a hemoglobin gene Hb^e, Hb^c, or thalassemia, or who are G6PD deficient are better able to survive in malarial environments. Malaria appears to be the selective force which maintains a balanced polymorphism for these traits, just as it presumably does for Hb^s gene. However, the anemia associated with these variants tends to be milder than sickle-cell anemia. The exception is thalassemia major, which causes a fatal form of anemia if the condition is not treated. This variation in degree of anemia may account for the difference in distribution of the genes for these conditions and for their association with particular kinds of malaria.

Distribution of Red-Cell Variants

Evidence to support the relationships between thalassemia, G6PD and malaria is provided by a study carried out on the island of Sardinia, once an intensely malarious area. A clear inverse correlation was found between altitude and frequency of thalassemia and G6PD deficiency (see Figure 5-5). At the higher elevations, as one moves away from the coastal plain, the rate of malarial infection decreases and there are fewer carriers of the genes for G6PD and thalassemia. Several villages, however, do not fit the correlations; endemic malaria is present but there is low thalassemia and G6PD deficiency in Carloforte and Usini. These exceptions can be explained by historical events. Both villages were established within the

FIGURE 5-5

Incidence of G6PD Deficiency and of the Thalassaemia Trait in Relation to Altitude Above Sea-Level

(From Siniscalco, 1966)

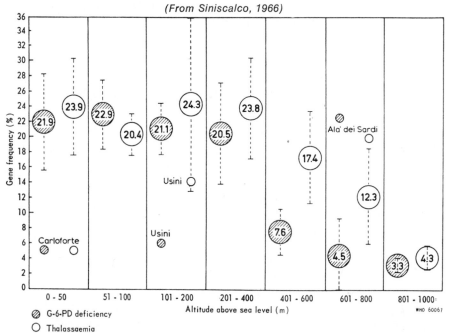

The figures in each of the large circles are the averages of the gene frequencies found in the villages that fall within the ending altitude groupings (0–50 meters, 51–100 meters, etc.).

last 200 years by populations from nonmalarious areas; hence, there has not been enough time for selective force to exert its influence on the gene frequency of these groups (Siniscalco et al., 1966).

The presence of Hb^s in high frequencies wherever falciparum is endemic is another such correlation that is worthy of note. Populations with over 15 percent gene frequency for Hb^s are known from West Africa to North East India or Eastern Pakistan (now Bangladesh), and in each of these areas falciparim malaria is transmitted continuously throughout the year. The question of the origin of this Hb^s gene outside the African continent logically comes up, since it has been considered by many to have originated in Africa. In many areas of the Mediterranean there is historical evidence of contact with Arab populations, who had established colonies in many places along its northern shores in Spain, Italy, Sicily, and Greece. African slaves from sub-Saharan areas were often brought in, and it is likely that at least some of them were carriers of the Hb[s] gene. In India, trade and some colonization are known to have occurred, and the same importation of the Hb[s] gene may have taken place.

However, it is difficult to explain the presence of such a high frequency of Hb[s] in certain parts of India solely on the basis of the importation of slaves (see Figure 5-6). There is a possibility that such a gene as

FIGURE 5-6

Hemoglobin S and Other Red-Cell Defects in India
(After Livingstone, 1967)

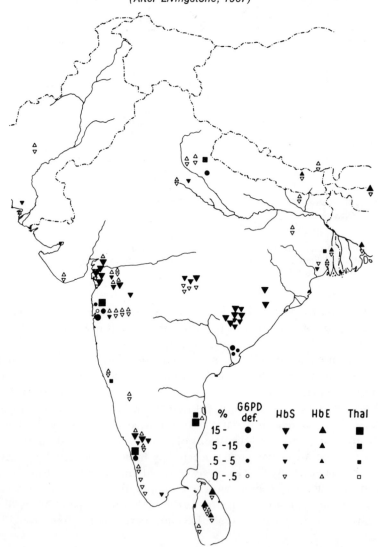

Hb^s, which is advantageous under certain conditions, appeared in several populations throughout human history by random mutations. The gene then would become fixed at high frequencies because of its advantage under conditions of endemic malaria. Such occurrence of spontaneous mutations would rule out the need to associate a particular gene with a particular race. However, the question is far from settled, and there are supporters for both sides of the argument: for gene distribution by migration and for random mutation. One group explains that a few mutations in a central area initiated an advantageous gene such as Hb^s, and from that central area, supposedly in the highlands of East Africa, the gene spread by population migration and interpopulation contact. However, such a scheme would make it difficult to explain how the gene arrived in remoter areas noncontiguous with the main African homeland, such as East Pakistan. The wide distribution of other red-cell abnormalities is equally difficult to explain. The hypothesis that several of the major red-cell defects are adaptive remains the most acceptable explanation for their high frequencies.

NATURAL SELECTION
AND THE BLOOD GROUPS

Unless the blood groups are adaptive, they are not going to be very useful in racial classification. Are they adaptive? At first glance, it doesn't look as if it made any difference what blood group one belongs to. (Boyd, 1963: 1057)

The distribution of the ABO allele frequencies vary widely throughout the world (Table 4-2). This uneven distribution suggests that natural selection has been operating to limit the A and B alleles to a frequency below 50 percent in a majority of the populations tested (see Figure 5-7). Alice Brues (1954, 1963) argued that such a distribution could most adequately be explained by balanced polymorphism at the ABO locus, which was maintained by selection for the heterozygote. Though the nature of the selection has yet to be fully understood, many workers now believe that the ABO alleles are adaptive and in some way influence survival, a factor that must be taken into account as noted in the quotation above.

An enormous amount of work has gone into an effort to discover natural selection at the ABO locus. Since the initial discovery of the ABO system in 1900, many millions of persons around the world have been typed, and extensive research has been carried on in an attempt to discover correlations between blood type and the incidence of disease. The results

The Adaptive Significance of Man's Variation

FIGURE 5-7

**Limits to the Range of Alleles A and B
in the World's Populations**

(After Brues, 1954)

PERCENT OF GENE A

PERCENT OF GENE B	0–5	5–10	10–15	15–20	20–25	25–30	30–35	35–40	40–45	45–50	50–55	55–60
0–5	6	7	1	2	4	3	3	2	1		1	
5–10	1	1	4	7	10	11	7	1	1	1		
10–15	1	2	8	13	15	16	8	1				
15–20			1	4	13	10	9	2				
20–25				2	9	6	2					
25–30				2	7	6	2	1				
30–35	1				2	2						
35–40												

Quantitative distribution of 215 representative human populations in respect to frequencies of the ABO blood group genes.

have been inconclusive, but they have stimulated much speculation about the meaning of blood-group polymorphism in all of the red-cell antigens and the ABO blood groups in particular.

Though the search for the meaning of blood-group polymorphisms over more than a half century has been disappointing, a number of possible explanations have emerged. These explanations can be grouped into several categories of selection that act to regulate allele frequencies over the period of human evolution and differentiation. Selection in man will function to cause differential fertility, differential mortality, and infant mortality in particular. There have been reports which describe that the ABO system is effective in all of these categories.

Differential Fertility

There was a significant difference in the rate of live births of type O mothers, and these women produced significantly fewer children when the fathers were type A or B. Further, if the male parent was heterozygous AO or BO, then there was a significantly greater number of OO children produced by the type O mother. The net result of matings incompatible for the ABO system is seen in Table 5-1.

The differential fertility acts in the following ways. First, there is a selection at the *prezygotic* stage. In a type O female there appears to be a greater chance of fertilization by the sperm carrying the type O gene, so the genotypes differ significantly from the expected frequency shown by the Hardy-Weinberg equilibrium, as in the following:

$$AO \quad \times \quad OO$$

AO   OO   (greater than 50 percent)

This selection for one male gamete over the other may be due to the antibodies in vaginal secretions, which will react with sperm specific for type A. Sperm have been shown to possess specific antigen reactions, but the question still remains of whether such specificity is due to the alleles carried by the sperm.

The second reason for reduction of fertility of incompatible matings is fetal loss due to antibodies A and B in the type O mother. These antibodies are small enough to pass easily through placental membranes, and they can enter the fetal bloodstream. Once there, they can disrupt fetal development and cause fetal death. Overall, several studies show that women who carry fetuses with ABO blood types incompatible with their own have a greater risk of fetal loss. The ease with which the antibodies from the maternal system can pass into the fetal bloodstream presents a clear danger similar to that known to exist for Rh hemolytic disease, though it occurs early in fetal development. These factors, prezygotic selection and fetal-maternal incompatibility lead to a lower fertility rate.

TABLE 5-1

ABO Blood Type and Fertility

(Based on Matsunaga, and Itoh, 1958, 1962)

	Matings where the ABO blood types of male and female are:	
	Compatible	Incompatible
Total matings	812	617
Pregnancies	2639	1928
Abortions*	273 (.10 per pregnancy)	295 (.15 per pregnancy)
Living Children*	2108	1341
Couples Childless*	80 (.10)	112 (.18)
Couples as yet infertile*	66 (.08)	72 (.12)

*These differences between compatible and incompatible matings are statistically significant.

Another result of incompatible matings, hemolytic disease, will be considered further on.

Differential Mortality and Disease

It was once supposed that certain ABO blood types were more susceptible to some diseases. These first associations were made with several chronic diseases, and a number of correlations were found (Table 5-2). The correlations indicated that persons of some blood types are more likely to suffer from a particular disease. The associations listed here are based on an analysis of thousands of hospital case histories and are statistically valid to the extent that they show a significant relationship, but the actual causal relationship between disease and red-cell antigens is not known. However, a significant number of gastrointestinal diseases are associated with the ABO antigens.

The presence of soluble antigens (ABH) in a majority of people plus the fact that many food substances, once broken down into molecular constituents, have a specific reaction with the ABO substances make it highly probable that there is a complex series of reactions between antigens and macromolecules within the gastrointestinal tract. Many of these reactions may enhance digestion or retard it, depending on the substances involved, or there may be chronic irritation of the fine mucous linings of the intestines. At any rate, it is more than a coincidence that many of the diseases associated with the ABO system are localized within the digestive system. Given the wide variety of foods that omnivorous *H. sapiens* can and has subsisted on for many thousands of years, the digestive system would be a logical focal point for natural selection.

TABLE 5-2
The ABO Blood Group and Chronic Diseases
(After Cavalli-Sforza and Bodmer, 1971; based on Clarke, 1961)

Disease	Mean Relative Incidence[a]		Chi-Square[b]
Duodenal ulcer	1.4	O:A, B and AB	200
Cancer of the stomach	1.25	A:O	49
Pernicious anemia	1.5	A:O	17
Stomach ulcer	1.82	O:A, B and AB	37
Cancer of the pancreas	1.27	A:O and B	8

[a]The mean relative incidence is the ratio of, for example, O:A in diseased patients divided by O:A in a control series.

[b]The x^2 for one degree of freedom tests the overall significance of the association, pooling all available data.

These chronic diseases have been used as evidence to demonstrate the correctness of original hypotheses that selection has been acting to influence polymorphisms of the ABO system. Note, however, that these diseases are of the type that usually afflict an individual later in adult life, near the end of his reproductive period. It is unlikely, then, that ulceration, diabetes, or cancer is going to influence a person's reproductive fitness. However, dietary-antigen relationships should be looked at carefully as an area of strong environmental influence.

Infectious diseases offer several interesting possibilities for explanation of the adaptability of blood groups. It has been argued that certain blood types cause the individual to be more susceptible to disease-causing organisms. Several relationships between the diseases listed in Table 5-3 have been offered as possibilities.

The organisms that cause these diseases have been demonstrated to be similar, antigenically, to either the A, B, or H antigens; that is, they have chemical structures on their outer coatings very similar in form to the antigens on the surface of the red blood cells. The explanation follows that the more similarity between the chemical structures of disease organisms and ABH antigens, the less likely is the individual's defense system to make antibodies against the disease organism. Thus the *Variola virus* (smallpox) has a chemical specificity similar to type A antigen. A person with type A blood would be more susceptible to smallpox than an O or B type. The findings of Vogel and his associates (Vogel, 1968) describe a mortality of 50 percent in type A persons (approximately four times higher than in B or O persons) among populations in India. As a matter of fact, the frequency of A is much lower among populations of the Indian subcontinent than among Europeans (see Figure 5-8). The bacteria, Pasteurella pestus (plague) is also considered to be more deadly to type O individuals, and when one considers the rate of mortality from this disease during the middle ages, when up to 90 percent of the populations of some

TABLE 5-3

ABO Blood and Infectious Diseases

Disease	*Reported Susceptibility in Blood Type*
Bronchial pneumonia	A
Filaria parasitic infection	A
Influenza	Probably O
Plague	O
Smallpox	A
Staphylococci infection	A
Streptococci infection	A and O
Typhoid	A

FIGURE 5-8

Distribution of Blood Type B in India
(Based on Buchi, 1968)

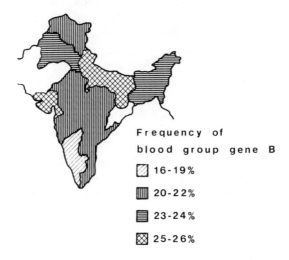

Frequency of
blood group gene B
◪ 16-19%
▦ 20-22%
▤ 23-24%
⊠ 25-26%

cities were wiped out, the effectiveness of the disease as a selective agent can be appreciated.

The areas of the world where plague has the longest history are the very areas where type O is found at the lowest frequency today. Areas which suffered from many outbreaks of the epidemic have a proportionately higher A and B frequency than regions where plague has never been reported or has been absent for several hundred years, as in Western Europe. Vogel points to Central Asia, India, and Mesopotamia as major plague centers, areas where populations have the lowest frequency of O. However, the extremely high B frequency and low O in Northern Siberian tribes has yet to be explained.

Recent studies have demonstrated that mosquitos have preferences in the blood types they choose to feed on. Volunteers were used to record the frequency of bites, and those persons with type O blood were bitten more often than type A or B. Should subsequent studies support these preliminary results, then malaria and other mosquito-borne diseases may be added to the list of disease selection at the ABO locus.

A glance at the chart of infectious diseases in Table 5-3 shows that many are of the type commonly found in larger populations who live in close contact in dense settlements and who are subjected to pollution of water and food supplies. One is tempted to speculate that only in recent times has selection operated to produce the ranges of gene-frequency variation for the ABO blood types—since the Neolithic, when man developed agriculture and adapted to settled village life. Supporting evidence is provided by the fact that the more isolated groups, especially those that have only recently (in the last few hundred generations) been involved with the development of dense sedentary life styles, are the ones with the highest type A frequencies—groups such as the Northwest Europeans. The Basques of Northern Spain, Lapps, Australian Aborigines, and Polynesians are some examples of isolation and high A frequencies.

The populations whose ancestors established the earliest large, densely populated, agriculturally based communities are those with the lowest A frequency (American Indian groups excepted). A majority of India's populations (see Figure 5-8), Siamese, and many Mideastern groups illustrate this relationship. This offers only a speculation based on the diverse data of the reactions between the red-cell antigens of the ABO and several diseases. The problem is a highly complex one; some selective forces may be acting in opposition to each other, as in the case of smallpox and plague, but the net effect is to alter a breeding population's gene combinations.

With all the information that we possess on the blood groups, explanations for their adaptive significance still escape us, and scant attention is given to natural selection in several recent authoritative works on the human blood groups. However, as Vogel (1968: 366) states, the blood-group antigens probably played an important role in man's evolution and adaptation:

> In earlier centuries, infections have killed a high percentage of mankind before reproductive age. Hence, selective pressure was very strong, and genetic adaptation to infections must have strongly influenced our present gene pool.

Infant mortality is the area where selection can be most influential in shaping the gene pool of future generations, especially when the high rate of infant deaths among primitive peoples is considered—over 50 percent in some populations. Often these deaths are due to various forms of gastrointestinal ailments or infant diarrhea, which is especially severe in populations who must make use of polluted water sources.

Differences in reactions of the blood type with several kinds of intestinal bacteria have been noted. This affects infants severely, since type A persons are more susceptible to certain types of infant diarrhea and hence suffer a higher mortality rate. Involvement of the ABO antigens with bacteria in the intestinal tract has been described, and there is no more critical period than when an infant is adjusting to the microbial groups common to his environmental setting. This period, and the period of stress on the young child's system during weaning, are times of extreme selection. Add to this all of the parasites and amebas found in many tropical regions, plus marginal diets, and one can easily see that any difference in susceptibility to infection, even though slight, will lead to extensive differences in mortality rates.

These are but a few possible demonstrations of the adaptive significance of the human ABO blood types. The other blood groups do not appear to be involved in an interaction with the environment; at least nothing is known about the action of natural selection on the several blood groups. There has been an excess of MN genotypes reported in

FIGURE 5-9

Percentage Frequency of Blood-Type Allele r (RH negative)
(After Hulse, 1971)

| ABSENT | 1-9 | 10-19 | 20-29 | 30-39 | 40-49 | 50+ | UNKNOWN |

some populations, but the significance of this greater-than-expected MN frequency over MM, NN genotypes is not known. The knowledge that man has no antibodies for this system does not aid our understanding. It should be recalled, also, that the M and N genes are evenly distributed throughout the world, excepting American Indians, who have a much greater frequency of M, while Australian Aborigines have high type N.

The distribution of genes of the Rh system suggests that a strong selection has been acting (see Figure 5-9). Figure 5-10 shows the reduction of the d allele, the gene responsible for 95 percent of the hemolytic disease in the newborn, under various conditions of selection. When selection against the allele is strongest, gene frequency approaches zero in a few generations. Since d allele persists at high frequency in several populations, some sort of selection must be acting to counteract the losses of the allele due to the hemolytic disease; perhaps selection favors the heterozygote.

Of the other blood groups two are worthy of note because of their peculiar distribution. The *Duffy group* shows a significant difference between Europeans and West Africans; according to Race and Sanger (1968: 341) this group provides the greatest distinction between the two populations of all the blood groups; African populations have between 60

FIGURE 5-10

Effects of Selection on Frequencies of d, D Alleles
(After Cavalli-Sforza and Bodmer, 1971)

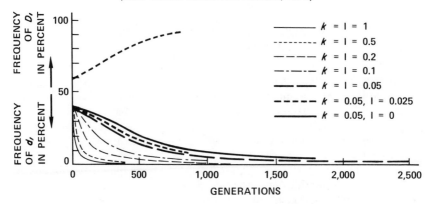

Change in the frequencies of rhesus alleles d (lower half of the figure) and D (upper half) with various values of the incompatibility selective coefficient k and l. Genotypes DD and Dd are Rh(+) and dd is Rh(−). The coefficient k measures selection against Dd in ♀dd × ♂DD matings, l measures selection in ♀dd × ♂Dd matings. Selection is absent when k and l are zero, in all cases an initial frequency of 0.4 for d is assumed.

and 90 percent of Fy (a—b—) while this allele is seldom found in Europeans (less than 35). Though interesting, this difference has no known significance.

The second blood group is the *Diego,* which is due to a simple dominant and is confined to Mongoloid peoples. The frequency of this allele is highest among certain South American Indians (36 percent) while virtually absent in Eskimos, though both have descended from Central Asian peoples. Some suggestion has been made that the gene, since it is most frequent in tropical populations, may in some way be adapted to that type of environment.

Finally, when all of the distributions of blood-group polymorphisms are considered and all explanations of selective forces are evaluated, definite adaptive value has not been established. It probably exists, because of the numerous interactions between environmental factors and blood types and because of the ways in which alleles differ between human populations. However, the reader must remember that allele frequencies are the end result of the sum total of several types of interactions, including natural selection. Additionally, though many blood types seem to be inherited as a single gene, it is likely that several if not all of the alleles for the different blood groups are pleiotropic; that is, they effect more than one phenotype. While the search continues for the survival value of the blood-group alleles, it is a reasonable assumption that diversity of these genes in our species is of adaptive value and has played a role in our evolution.

RECOMMENDED READINGS AND
LITERATURE CITED

ANGEL, J. L. 1966. "Porotic hyperostosis anemias, malarias and marshes in prehistoric eastern Mediterranean," *Science,* 153: 760–763.

BARNICOT, N. A. 1957. "Human pigmentation," *Man,* 57(144): 114–120.

BLUM, HAROLD F. 1962. "Does the melanin pigment of human skin have adaptive value? An essay in human ecology and the evolution of race.," *Quart. Rev. Biol.,* 36: 50–63.

BLUM, HAROLD F. 1969. "Is sunlight a factor in the geographical distribution of human skin color?," *The Geograph. Review,* vol. LIX, no. 4, pp. 557–581.

BOYD, WM. C. 1963. "Genetics and the human race," *Science,* 140: 1057–1064.

BRUES, A. M. 1954. "Selection and polymorphism in the ABO blood groups," *Am. J. Phys. Anthrop.,* 12: 559–597.

———. 1963. "Stochastic tests of selection in the ABO blood groups," *Am. J. Phys. Anthrop.,* 21(3): 287–300.

BUCHI, ERNST C. 1968. "Somatic groups composing the modern population of India," in *Proceedings Eighth International Congress of Anthropological and Ethnological Sciences.* Ueno Park, Tokyo, Japan: Science Council of Japan, pp. 154–162.

CAVALLI-SFORZA, L. L. and W. F. BODMER. 1971. *The Genetics of Human Populations.* San Francisco: W. H. Freeman & Co.

COON, CARLETON S. 1965. *The Living Races of Man.* New York: Alfred A. Knopf, Inc.

DOBZHANSKY, THEODOSIUS. 1971. "Race equality," in *The Biological and Social Meaning of Race,* Richard H. Osborne, ed. San Francisco: W. H. Freeman & Co., pp. 13–24.

HULSE, FREDERICK S. 1971. *The Human Species.* New York: Random House, Inc.

IVANHOE, FRANCIS. 1970. "Was Virchow right about Neanderthal?," *Nature,* 227: 577–579.

LIVINGSTONE, FRANK B. 1958. "Anthropological implications of sickle cell gene distribution in West Africa," *Am. Anthrop.,* 60(3): 533–562.

———. 1967. *Abnormal Hemoglobins in Human Populations.* Chicago: Aldine Publishing Co.

———. 1971. "Malaria and human polymorphisms," *Annual Review of Genetics,* 5: 33–64.

LOOMIS, F. W. 1967. "Skin-pigment regulation of vitamin D biosynthesis in man," *Science,* 157: 501–506.

———. 1970. *Rickets.* "Scientific American," 223(6): 77–91.

RACE, R. R. and R. SANGER. 1968. *Blood Groups in Man.* Philadelphia: F. A. Davis.

SINISCALCO, M., L. BERNINI, G. FILIPPI, B. LATTE, P. MEERA KHAN, S. PIOMELLI, and M. RATTAZZI. 1966. "Population genetics of haemoglobin variants, thalassemia and glucose-6-phosphate dehydrogenase deficiency with particular reference to the malaria hypothesis," *Bulletin Wld. Hlth. Org.,* 34: 379–393.

VOGEL, F. 1968. "Anthropological implications of the relationship between ABO blood groups and infections," *Proceedings Eighth International Congress of Anthropological and Ethnological Sciences,* 1: 365–370.

WALSH, R. J. 1963. "Variations of melanin pigmentation of the skin in some Asian and Pacific peoples," *Journal of the Royal Anthropological Inst.,* 93, pt. 1: 126–33.

chapter six

Human Variability and Behavior

Every racial group possesses all of the different genes which condition or impart the differing capacities to respond or adapt to the good and bad environments of our complex society. (Frederick Osborn, 1971: 155)

Equality or inequality of men has been disputed in our society and western civilization for many centuries. The notion that the differences which set other peoples apart from us are somehow indicative of an inferior being or a lesser human is of great antiquity. Despite the many thousands of pages written to refute these misbeliefs and to document the severe lack of data, these concepts of racial superiority and inferiority are, perhaps, as strong today as they ever were. Witness the recent rise of the studies that attempt to show intellectual inferiority of the American Negro and of statements which describe the "Negro race" as having a lower I.Q. because of the inheritance of "inferior" genes.

There is no need at this point to review those strongly held beliefs which associate a particular form of behavior with certain racial groups. We all have heard them many times. But consider: if there is a wide genetic diversity within each major geographic unit (race), which we have considered previously, then there should be an equally wide range of those genes related to man's behavior. Simply stated, there are "bright" and "dull" people in all groups of *H. sapiens.* Just as genetic distribution was not made understandable by clustering into major geographic units, so it is difficult or downright impossible to talk of "racial" variation of behavior. The problem is further complicated by the nature of the phenotype, a polygenic trait. Because of its complexity it is not possible to speak separately of genetically or environmentally determined behavior. It is far ·better to avoid stereotypes altogether and consider individual pedigrees when we study effects of genes on behavior.

Explanation of variability of the human phenotypes that are easily measured has proven difficult, as discussed throughout these pages, but discussion and comprehension of behavioral diversity is further complicated by the difficulties of measuring and labeling mental ability and behavior. The observer's culture greatly influences his judgment or perception, particularly if he is studying a primitive society which lacks a written language and whose people look and dress quite differently from those in the observer's own group. It takes many months or years to gain insight and understanding, and even then most observers are only partly successful. This means that any comparisons between the "native" and civilized minds is speculative at best and will reveal little about behavioral genetic diversity.

The American Negro has been the object of many studies, and the results have frequently been used in attempts to show that there is something innately inferior about this group. A certain number of their "behavior genes" are supposed to be inferior, and there is even a belief in certain circles that "the Negro has a gene for slow learning." Of course, there is no way for such a gene, if it even existed, to be identified. Even the detection of its presence in an individual is not possible, just as many polygenic traits have unknown gene combinations where the individual genes cannot be identified. About all that the many studies of the American Negro have shown is that, as a group, they have a lower I.Q., by a few points, than the white population. Much more has been made of this small difference than the data permit, especially when discussing genes, behavior, and race, because no control for gene admixture is ever made.

Few will deny that there are inherited behavioral differences between individuals, and that there is probably a significant biological component underlying our behavior responses. This biological component is perhaps best illustrated by the mental retardation which accompanies the several kinds of chromosome abnormalities. The Klinfelter (XXY sex chromosomes), Turner (XO), and Down's (mongolism) syndromes all possess mental defects among the general symptoms which result from an error in chromosome number. The doubts and controversy over genetic basis for behavior arise when, on the basis of very crude measures, these differences or distinctions, seen between individuals, are attributed to an entire group. Dividing race on the basis of inferior or superior attributes only feeds racial conflicts and prevents understanding of behavior-genetic variability.

Biochemical basis for behavior is an area scarcely touched by investigators, though there are several possibilities for explaining certain clinically defined mental illnesses in terms of enzyme defects. Whether or not these enzyme polymorphisms are more frequent in some groups than others remains to be determined. But, at any rate, there are many physiological variables that affect behavioral response to stimuli. Brain development is also affected, as in the case of the mental defects associated with the ability to metabolize phenylalamine (page 85). Poor nutrition also hampers brain development if it occurs in the early stages of growth—generally in the first year of postnatal life—and can result in a mentally retarded individual. Finally, we should consider that, unfortunately, the question of the influence of the genetic system on behavior is usually bound up with the sociopolitical question of "race."

RACE AND BEHAVIOR

The United States census of 1840 provided the "proof" that the supporters of slavery needed. The record showed that there were many times more Negroes in the North suffering from mental illness (1 in every 144) than in the South (1 in 1558). The conclusion was that the Negro lived happier and healthier under conditions of slavery than when he was given his freedom, as the "high insanity rate" among free Negroes in the North "proved." This record supported the generally held belief that racial mental inferiority was a fact, and the census report was widely quoted as evidence for many years. As soon as the census was published, a young doctor named Edward Jarvis attempted to get Congress to amend the census.[1] He showed that the entire report on mental illness was in error and that insane Negroes were reported in towns and cities which had no black residents at all or, in some cases, the number described as insane far exceeded the total. Jarvis' attempts to correct these errors were not successful, and the 1840 census continued to be cited for many years as a rationale for slavery.

Since the mid-nineteenth century many studies have been carried out, and several differences between Negro and white have been recorded. A higher frequency of psychosis was reported among Negroes, and their admissions to state hospitals for neurosis have been more frequent in certain states. Many careful surveys have shown that these differences,

[1] See Stanton, 1960.

however, are attributed to social factors rather than biological differences or deficiencies. Nonetheless, beliefs persist that intellectual ability and adaptability to modern society differ between races because of innate biological characteristics which each is supposed to possess. The following quotation illustrates this point.

> Nature has color-coded groups of individuals so that statistically reliable predictions of their adaptability to intellectually rewarding and effective lives can easily be made and profitably be used by the pragmatic man in the street. (Shockley, 1972: 307)

This quotation is difficult to refute—not because it states a fact but because it presents a timeless folklore dear to many. The flat statement of group differences based on simple visual appraisal has been used by man for perhaps as long as *H. sapiens* has existed as a species, and the refutation of such appraisals has been a major effort of this book. The division of man's cultural traits, his behavior, or some other facet of his being is a tempting exercise, since it ultimately simplifies the broad diversity that exists. The behavioral variety that appears to exist between races or ethnic groups is difficult if not impossible to attribute solely to a biological basis (the genes). Many of these so-called innate differences are actually due to cultural influences of language or socioeconomic status or to the physical environment.

The cultural component is responsible for a great deal of variability, and often cultures are evaluated as being modern or primitive, simple or complex. The behavior of individuals participating in a culture other than our own differs from what we have come to know as "standard" *H. sapiens'* behavior, particularly when the technology is primitive or simple, such as the Stone Age cultures of New Guinea or Australia. Rather than make a value judgment, it would be more logical and would aid understanding if each culture were considered as an adaptation to the environment in which it is found. Whether it be the rigorous environment of the Australian "outback," which nurtures the Stone-Age culture of the Aborigine, or the impoverished peoples in an urban ghetto, the socio-cultural framework enables the maintenance of human society.

When we consider language, we find a great deal of complexity even in so-called primitive cultures. Rather than measure mental capacity or sociabiltiy on the basis of doubtful testing procedures, we might do better to look at the communication system and determine how each group copes with the demands of its environment. If one sees languages as a basis for human behavior and as necessary foundations for society, then the investigator is forced to the conclusion that, while there are individual differences in mental capacity, all groups appear to be equal in their capacities and their intellectual ability to respond to the challenges of the environment.

Many times in the past, in the study of primitive societies, assumptions have been made by the investigator about the capacity of the people to deal with—in our terms—more complex or abstract subjects. Invariably, these assumptions proved to be wrong. The world view, individual experiences, society's behavioral roles, and physical environment often proved to be the deciding factors. Misunderstanding of the society and its culture often led to statements such as: "Inadequate neurological organization has been a major factor in the origin and persistence of a fundamental cultural inadequacy—lack of written communication." (Green, 1967: 26) This study attributed improper neurological development to the techniques of child rearing, particularly where the infant is restrained, as on a cradle board, and not permitted to crawl. The investigator studied a limited number of Amazonian Indians and several African groups and reached his conclusions without taking into account the many other variables and diversity within the cultures studied. Had he studied these groups more carefully, his conclusions might be quite different.

No doubt there is a considerable amount of inherited behavior variability among individuals. But what is highly questioned is the grouping of these differences into the gross categories which we have spent so much time discussing—race.

POPULATION, RACE, AND BEHAVIOR

> Blessed are the statistical tables, for they delay the day of our thinking. . . . Run your eye down the rows of books on population published in the last ten years. Lose yourself in the thickets of tables of numbers. Is all this necessary? Is the population problem really so subtle? Are we unable to get along without this dissimulation of reality and the fatigue of prolixity that puts an end to genuine inquiry? (Hardin, 1963: 366)

Hardin made this comment in a criticism of those who endlessly argue over statistical details without really dealing with the key question of population growth and overcrowding. We are not concerned at this point with the question of size and growth but with the uncritical use of race as a label, a means of stereotyping behavior. Hardin's statement, however, points out the often needless confusion that surrounds the problem of population composition and the overreliance on statistical abstractions. The following statement by Jensen (1971: 16–17) provides an example:

> Although most of the studies of racial differences in intelligence are based on social definitions of race, it should be noted that there is usually a high correlation between the social and the biological definitions, and it is most unlikely that results of the research would be very different if the investigators had used biological rather than social criteria of race in selecting groups for comparison.

The use of social stereotypes of ethnic groups may be acceptable for some purposes, but in any attempt to study the genetic system a careful distinction must be made for population composition. Use of a social classification of a group based on a known attribute generally ignores all others, as in the case of American Negroes. Their ancestry is quite mixed, comprising from 10 to 90 percent Caucasoid genes, with the average given as 20 to 30 percent. In addition, the African ancestry is anything but homogeneous (see Alland, 1971, and Reed, 1969). African populations are as diverse as any in the world (see page 54), and the American Negro's African ancestry consists of a contribution from a variety of these populations. Slaves imported into Charleston, South Carolina, between 1733 and 1807 were from a region ranging from Senegambia to Angola, an area of 1000 × 600 miles, which covers a variety of environment and a diversity of cultures.

If for no other reason, criticism of studies of racial differences in intelligence can be made on these grounds: that these studies are often carried out on groups where the actual genetic composition is not known. Nor is the group distinguished or identified as a breeding population; and its recent ancestry and history are ignored. The only concern often is with the social definition of "race"—again pointing out the error and the handicap of the confusion of culture and biological variables.

It is one thing to discuss genetic potential, gene frequency, or inherited ability within a breeding population whose members share a large number of genes in common; it is another, quite different matter to discuss these variables in reference to "race" (socially or biologically defined). The claim is often made that an admixture of Caucasoid genes actually causes an increased I.Q. in American Negroes, as if Caucasoids were a homogeneous group all possessing the same gene combination, regardless of whether northern or southern, eastern or western European in origin. Such statements on admixture and I.Q. are unfounded; data do not exist to support such a contention. Correlations can be made between combinations of genes and behavior only when the ancestry and genetic admixture of each individual tested are known; and only when breeding-population boundaries are established can interpopulation comparisons be made. These are difficult criteria to fulfill, of course, but any study that purports to examine genotypes and the behavioral phenotype must carefully determine population composition. Anything less will produce misleading data.

THE INHERITANCE OF I.Q.

> While it certainly is true that I started out to study the genetics of a behavior, in the course of much thinking and experimenting over more than a decade I have come to realize that it is impossible to study the genetics of a behavior. We can study the behavior of *an* organism, the genetics of *a* population, and individual differences in the expression of some behavior by members of *that* population. (Hirsch, 1969: 43)

Among the many polygenic traits of man, behavioral responses, or intellectual capacity, are among the most difficult to deal with. Not only is little known about the genetics influencing behavior, but extreme difficulty is encountered when attempts are made to identify or label the phenotypes. Witness the disagreement over what I.Q. is and the wide variation in diagnosis of mental illness or behavioral pathologies in our society. Given these factors, it is much more difficult to establish genetic relationships for behavior than for polygenic phenotypes such as skin color, face form, or stature. Since we are not concerned here with phenotypic labeling of "types" or behavior, we will look only at the methods employed to determine the degree of genetic influence on the performance of standard I.Q. tests.

Heritability

Variance, the degree of variation about the mean value for a trait in a population (the standard deviation squared), is due to the influences of both the environment and the genes. The variance in the environment plus the variance in the genotypes is equal to the variance in the phenotype $(V_p = V_g + V_e)$; this equation means that if the environment is constant or equal for all individuals in a population, then any variance in phenotypes will be due to a variance in genotypes in the population. Heritability is that proportion of population variance attributable to genetic factors. It is described by the formula

$$H^2 = \frac{V_g}{V_g + V_e},$$

which is a simple statement that H^2 represents the ratio of genetic variance to total variance. From this formula it is obvious that a phenotype which has a high degree of variance due to genetic variance within the population would have a high H^2.

Heritability is not a measure of the genetics of a phenotype; it is merely a measure of the total effect of the genotype variance on phenotypic variability. As described by Gregg and Sanday (1971: 59): "Heritability only tells what proportion of the variance is due to genetic differences, not the extent to which a trait is determined by genetic factors." Additionally, heritability is not a constant value that tells us the degree of genetic influence on the phenotype of any single individual. As stated by Jensen (1971: 13–14):

> There is no single true value of the heritability of a trait. Heritability is not a constant, but a population statistic, and it can vary according to the test used and the particular population tested.

If the example is used of a group of individuals placed on a diet which contains a carefully controlled constant amount of phenylalanine (the $V_e = 0$), then any variance of phenylalanine blood levels (the V_p in the population) will be due to V_g or a variance in the genetic system. If later the diet is varied between members of the same group, then phenotypic variance will increase. This does not mean that the genetic contributors or the effects of the genes is any less, merely that the ratios $(V_g/V_p) + (V_e/V_p) = 1$ change. In neither case is the degree of genetic contribution or gene effect known.

H^2 of a phenotypic variance within a population tells us nothing about the genetic component in the individual; what it does describe is the degree of variance in a population which is due to the genes under a certain set of environmental circumstances. This simple formula actually describes a method employed by animal and plant breeders long before genetic inheritance was known or understood. Farmers could selectively breed their stock by the simple logic that any variation in animals living under a stable environment (the same food, pasturage, and so on) was due to some factors of inheritance ("blood lines") that could be passed on to the next generation. This way undesirable traits could be selected out and useful traits bred for. The egg producers in a flock of chickens, cows who produced the most milk, or cattle that showed the greatest weight gain could be used as breeders. The genetics were not known (and in many cases still are a mystery), but desirable effects of selective breeding could easily be seen, evaluated, and used to advantage.

Heritability studies are useful as a predictive device in animal husbandry and show what can be done under conditions of artificial selection. They are useful, however, only when confined to the breeding population under study, and the ratio of V_g to V_e is not the same for other populations. In the case of man many complications arise, because it is not possible to control human breeding or to regulate and select as in nonhuman populations.

Twin Studies

To overcome the difficulties of determining genetic-environment influences in man, studies of monozygous or identical twins offer a ready source of information. Correlations or similarities of phenotypes of twins raised together and those raised separately offer a means of estimating heritability. This has been especially applied to estimates of heritability of intelligence. Table 6-1 shows that MZ (monozygous) twins raised together are most similar (correlation of 0.87), while parent-child groups have a correlation of 0.50. Presumably, the similarities are due to genotypes shared by related individuals. In the case of the 0.20 correlation between foster parent and child, similarities of I.Q. are due to a sharing of the home environment.

In order to gain the H^2 ratio from the correlation coefficient of phenotypes of MZ twins raised apart, one assumes that any differences in phenotypes are due to environmental variances. Therefore, since the correlations are due to genetic similarity, $H^2 = r$, the correlation coefficient. Available twin studies, roughly 122 groups of MZ twins since 1925, give H^2 estimates for correlations in I.Q. ranging from 60 to 90 percent with an average of 80 percent. Several difficulties with these twin studies have been pointed out; two problems are most prominent. First, most of these studies were made over thirty years ago, when controls, questions, and methods were somewhat different than today. Second, there is a wide difference in the time of separation of the twins. Most were separated between 2 months and 2 years of age, but the range is 1 month to 6 years, which increases the problem of sorting out environmental influences.

No matter what data are used nor how carefully the study was made in one population, the H^2 estimate could not be extended to estimates in other populations, which certainly would differ in genotypes or environment, probably both. However, frequently we read statements that claim human intelligence, as measured by standard tests, is due 80 percent to influence of man's gene.

We are faced with a dilemma here. H^2 gives a ratio of genetic influence to environmental influence, but it does not mean that environment does not have an effect even when H^2 is large. In the formula $V_p = V_g + V_e$ no allowance is made for the uniform factors in the environment, which may be constant and may not contribute to variance but will affect

TABLE 6-1
Correlations for Intellectual Ability: Obtained and Theoretical Values
(From Jensen, 1969)

Correlations Between	Number of Studies	Obtained Median r[a]	Theoretical Value[b]	Theoretical Value[c]
Unrelated Persons				
Children reared apart	4	-0.01	0.00	0.00
Foster parent and child	3	+0.20	0.00	0.00
Children reared together	5	+0.24	0.00	0.00
Collaterals				
Second Cousins	1	+0.16	+0.14	+0.063
First Cousins	3	+0.26	+0.18	+0.125
Uncle (or aunt) and nephew (or niece)	1	+0.34	+0.31	+0.25
Siblings, reared apart	33	+0.47	+0.52	+0.50
Siblings, reared together	36	+0.55	+0.52	+0.50
Dizygotic twins, different sex	9	+0.49	+0.50	+0.50
Dizygotic twins, same sex	11	+0.56	+0.54	+0.50
Monozygotic twins, reared apart	4	+0.75	+1.00	+1.00
Monozygotic twins, reared together	14	+0.87	+1.00	+1.00
Direct Line				
Grandparent and grandchild	3	+0.27	+0.31	+0.25
Parent (as adult) and child	13	+0.50	+0.49	+0.50
Parent (as child) and child	1	+0.56	+0.49	+0.50

[a] Correlations not corrected for attenuation (unreliability).

[b] Assuming assortative mating and partial dominance.

[c] Assuming random mating and only additive genes—that is, the simplest possible polygenic model.

the expression of the phenotype. In other words, no matter what estimate is given for the proportion of variance due to V_g, even if it is unity, environment is still interacting with the genotypes to form the phenotype. Further, just because an H^2 of 0.80 is measured for several groups of twins does not mean that this is a ratio universally applicable to any other group or population.

Of all the great many twin studies made throughout the years in an attempt to learn the relative influences of environment and genetics a recent and most comprehensive study was reported by Scarr-Salapatek (1971), who described results on 992 pairs of monozygous twins in Philadelphia. This study pointed out several important factors regarding the relative influences of environment and genetics. First, and perhaps chief among the results, was that 75 percent of the total variance on test scores of whites was due to genetic variance, while the proportion of genetic variance in disadvantaged black populations was less. This provides evidence for the correctness of the statement that studies of twins as a method of obtaining H^2 is not fully dependable for the general population, since twins are not a representative group of the general population.

Scarr-Salapatek tested the hypothesis that "Social class differences in phenotypic I.Q. are assumed to reflect primarily the mean differences in genotype distribution by social class; environmental differences between social class groups (and races) are seen as insignificant in determining total phenotypic variance in I.Q." (1971: 1286). She found, through extensive black and white twin comparisons, that environment played an important role in variance and that the hypothesis of genetic differences as a base for I.Q. differences was incorrect.

Many of the differences or variations are even more interesting than the similarities (see Figure 6-1). Twins raised apart have up to 20 points difference, which again shows effect of environment. Adopted children show a gain of 20 points over their biological mothers, and the correlation between parents and children is approximately 0.5, but bright parents usually have children with lower I.Q., which is described as regression towards the mean. If all of these factors are considered, there is a basic error in the argument that lower I.Q.'s among certain groups are due to genetic differences.

We are dealing with a complex combination of genes when we consider mental ability, and the polygenic nature of this phenotype means that a considerable number of interactions occur between genes, their products, and environment. It is misleading to attempt to partition relative influence of environment and genetics in such a complex organism as man. The nature of much of the genetic system is its potential to interact with environmental stimuli. A gene-enzyme response syndrome is an example, and the level of the enzymatic response is probably a result

FIGURE 6-1

Effects of Environment

(From Cavalli-Sforza and Bodmer, 1970)

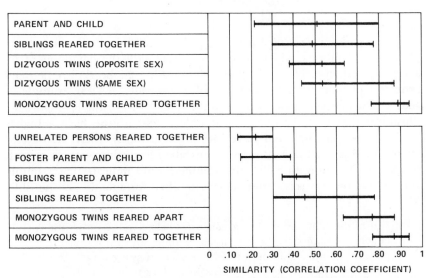

Effects of environment can be measured by comparing correlation coefficients of individuals with similar genetic backgrounds reared in different environments and those with different backgrounds reared in the same environment. Published data collected by Erlenmeyer-Kimling and Jarvik show that unrelated persons reared together have coefficients that range from about 0.15 to slightly over 0.30. Coefficients for foster parents and children range from 0.16 to almost 0.40. Siblings reared apart have coefficients that range from more than 0.30 to more than 0.40. Siblings reared together have coefficients that range from 0.30 to almost 0.80. Monozygous twins reared apart have coefficients that range from more than 0.60 to above 0.80, and monozygous twins reared together have coefficients of more than 0.70 to more than 0.90. It appears that environment affects intelligence but not as strongly as heredity does.

of the storage of information. The central nervous system stores and retrieves information as an adaptation to the environment, and a feedback loop is formed. The cultural environment, the genes, and stored experience all provide a mental template which will vary from population to population.

It is a truism that behavior cannot be biologically inherited but must be developed and elicited under the combined influence of genetic and environmental factors. The effects of genes must be expressed

through physiological action, and it has long been known that genes
modify each other's effects so that only when a gene has a major and
usually disruptive effect is there a one-to-one relationship between
gene and character. (Scott, 1969: 64)

The genes determine a product, perhaps enzymes that express some
physiological process, which in turn interacts with the environment by
a certain response. No one single relationship can be shown between
gene and phenotype in the case of polygenic traits. A clear example of
gene-product-enzyme action is seen in the case of PKU patients. Figure 6-2
illustrates that those carrying the double recessive gene have a higher
level of phenylalanine and have low I.Q. Obviously, there are several
factors involved, such as dietary phenylalanine during various growth
periods. In addition, though, this example should indicate that a simple
application of any correlation or heritability formula is not possible.

Just as the value assigned to a particular behavioral characteristic is
largely determined by the circumstances under which it is called into
play, the nature and form in which the characteristic emerges are not
predetermined and fixed but are products of a genotype-environment
interaction. (Gordon, 1969: 70)

GENETICS, INTELLIGENCE,
AND THE FUTURE

The final, definitive research must await a racially integrated America
in which opportunities are the same for both races. . . . The important conclusion for the present, however, is that if there are any
inherent distinctions, they are inconsequential. Even now, differences
in I.Q. within any one race greatly exceed the differences between
the races. Race as such is simply not an accurate way to judge an
individual's intelligence. (Pettigrew, 1971: 116)

For many decades we have been warned of the possibility of a
decline in human intelligence because of disproportionate breeding of
certain segments in our society. But the prediction that collective intelligence would decrease 1 to 4 points per generation has proven to be
false. For a time it looked like an accurate prediction, since the "least
intelligent" appeared to be producing more children, but longitudinal

FIGURE 6-2

Frequency Distributions of Some Characteristics of Phenylketonuria (PKU) in PKU Patients (Shaded) and in Control Populations
(Redrawn from L. S. Penrose, 1951)

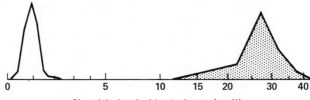

Phenylalanine in blood plasma (mg %)

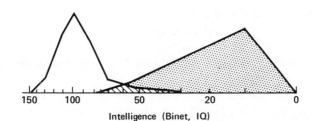

Intelligence (Binet, IQ)

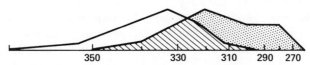

Head size.   Length + breadth in mm (corrected for sex)

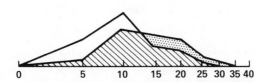

Hair color. Reflectance % at 700 mμ (corrected for age)

Hair color and head size show pronounced overlap, and intelligence shows some overlap. The level of phenylalanine in the blood, however, is higher in all PKU patients than in controls. If intelligence were the only phenotype used in the analysis, the genotype would be said to be nonpenetrant in a small proportion of cases. When plasma level of phenylalanine is the phenotype, the genotype is found to be fully penetrant.

data have shown that there has been no decline in general intelligence. In fact, the often expressed concern about birth rates among low-I.Q. groups is based on early studies which showed women with low I.Q. had more children, but the studies did not count the women who never had children. This, of course, resulted in an incorrect estimate of fertility among low-I.Q. groups. Actually, since many women of this group never have children, the result of comparison of fertility of the two groups is that the reproductive rate of the high-I.Q. group is greater. The many factors operating to maintain the species I.Q. mean are not known, but they appear to balance out as natural selection operates to select for those individuals that fit best within our complex society. Assortative mating, differential birth rates, marriage rates, and institutionalization are all part of the scheme.

The measure of mental ability or I.Q. differences between social groups (or racial groups) has been questioned many times and is often attributed to differences in a central theme involving survival and life styles. The basis for variance in I.Q. may lie in discriminatory practices, economics, and language. Groups consistently scoring lower on standardized tests do not necessarily come from an "inferior" environment but from one which is distinct from the environment of the group on which the test was originally standardized. The various tests were designed as predictive devices, and as such they work very well to a limited extent —but, unfortunately, people have tried to use them for other purposes. To be comparable, two persons taking the same test should have been exposed to the same material and experiences and be in the same state of physical development. Or, as Scarr-Salapatek stated (1971: 1287):

> Only if black children could be reared as though they were white, and vice versa, could the effects of different rearing environments on the genotype distribution of the two races be estimated.

Biological or social definition of race, controlled or modified tests—none of these matters in the preceding arguments so long as we assume that man is "color coded." It is dangerous and inaccurate to assume that if the variation of trait X in population A differs from the variation of the trait in population B, then all traits differ at the same rate between the two groups. "Races" are not inferior or superior; there is no "gene" for slow learning; and the genetics of whatever I.Q. is has yet to be determined. The future may look bleak to some who claim a decline in I.Q., but there are no data to demonstrate such a decline.

RACIAL DIFFERENCES AND I.Q.—
A MEASURE OF MENTAL ABILITY?

The argument rages on endlessly over what standardized tests for mental ability actually measure. With all of the millions of tests administered during this century no agreement has been reached as to what is actually tested. "Intelligence is what I.Q. tests measured," states one worker; "I.Q. tests measure learning experience," declares another. Whatever the test scores reveal about the individual, they are widely used in our society and often place individuals within a niche in our educational system. Such placement has far-reaching effects on a person's future development and achievement. The test scores of the individual vary 4 to 5 points upon retesting over short intervals, but over intervals of several years, variations of 20 to 30 points are known, supporting the belief that tests are a measure of learning and experience.

The normal distribution of I.Q. for a population whose mean is 100 represents a group which has been used as a standard for I.Q. scores— the American Middle Class—while comparison between this group and the American Negroes is shown in Figure 6-3. The 15-point difference is considered by many to be significant and by some as an indication of inherited differences.

What is striking about these curves is the range of variability, *not* the difference between the means. The variability in both could be explained by the fact that there is an extreme range of occupational differences and socioeconomic status in both groups. Hence the stimuli and learning experiences are quite diverse—doctors, lawyers, and so on occur in white and black samples, but a greater number of lower-economic-level groups are found in the Negro sample. Even in just these terms the differences of the mean could be explained, but there are many more reasons to be explored.

A major reason for I.Q. differences is educational advantage. A review of 20 of the 122 twins studies which ranked them for differences in educational advantage showed a correlation of 0.79 between I.Q. and educational advantage. Table 6-2 shows the relationship between test scores of army draftees and school expenditures; the more funds spent per child in the state, the higher the scores by young men of draft age a generation later. Figure 6-4 displays the differences between black and white. The middle sections of the graph, often attributed to genetic differences, vary widely from state to state depending on educational expenditures.

FIGURE 6-3

I.Q. Differences between Blacks and Whites in the United States

(From Cavalli-Sforza and Bodmer, 1970)

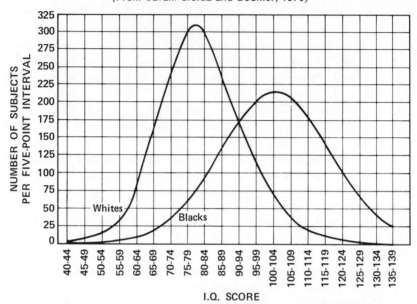

I.Q. difference between U.S. blacks and whites emerges from a comparison of the I.Q. distribution in a representative sample of whites with the I.Q. distribution among 1,800 black children in the schools of Alabama, Florida, Georgia, Tennessee and South Carolina. Wallace A. Kennedy of Florida State University, who surveyed the students' I.Q., found that the mean I.Q. of this group was 80.7. The mean I.Q. of the white sample is 101.8, a difference of 21.1 points. The two samples overlap distinctly, but there is also a sizable difference between the two means. Other studies show a difference of 10 to 20 points, making Kennedy's result one of the most extreme reported.

Factors relating to health also cause wide variation in I.Q. Early deafness is known to lower I.Q. by 20 points. Premature and underweight babies have lower I.Q. as measured at different developmental stages. Twins on the average are 5 points lower and triplets 9 points. Nutrition is known to play a major factor, as demonstrated by several programs which showed an increase in I.Q. of 8 to 10 points when the groups were fed an enriched diet.

The socioeconomic status of the parents affects greatly the I.Q. performance of the children, since there is a high correlation between S.E.S. and I.Q. When racial-ethnic groups scores are adjusted for social background, the I.Q. differences between groups are reduced from 15 points to 4 points. A rather intensive study of preschool children showed

TABLE 6-2

Median and Mean Negro and White Army Alpha Intelligence Test Scores and School Expenditures Per Child Aged 5 to 18 Years By State

(From Spuhler, 1967; data from Yerkes, 1921, and
Statistical Abstract of the United States, 1902)

	White			Negro			
State (1)	N (2)	Me-dian (3)	Mean (4)	N (5)	Me-dian (6)	Mean (7)	School expend-itures (8)
Alabama	779	41.3	49.4	271	19.9	27.0	1.51
Arkansas	710	35.6	43.3	193	16.1	22.6	3.09
Florida	55	53.8	59.8	499	9.2	15.3	4.68
Georgia	762	39.3	48.3	416	10.0	17.2	2.68
Illinois	2,145	61.6	66.7	804	42.2	47.9	13.46
Indiana	1,171	56.0	62.2	269	41.5	47.6	11.75
Kansas	861	62.7	67.0	87	34.7	40.6	10.58
Kentucky	837	41.5	48.6	191	23.9	32.4	4.57
Louisiana	702	41.1	49.0	538	13.4	20.8	2.52
Maryland	616	55.3	60.2	148	22.7	30.7	8.44
Mississippi	759	37.6	43.7	773	10.2	16.8	2.63
Missouri	1,329	56.5	61.9	196	28.3	34.2	8.54
New Jersey	937	45.3	52.9	748	33.0	38.9	14.04
New York	3,300	58.4	63.7	1,188	38.6	45.3	19.22
North Carolina	702	38.2	45.9	211	16.3	22.1	1.51
Ohio	2,318	67.2	73.0	163	45.4	53.4	12.13
Oklahoma	865	43.0	50.6	98	31.4	35.9	5.50
Pennsylvania	3,280	62.0	67.1	790	34.8	40.5	12.85
South Carolina	581	45.1	51.1	334	14.2	19.2	1.93
Tennessee	710	44.0	52.0	504	29.7	35.9	2.71
Texas	1,426	43.5	50.2	854	12.2	18.2	4.38
Virginia	506	56.3	60.5	57	45.6	52.0	3.39
West Virginia	423	54.9	60.8	67	26.8	28.5	6.79
Subtotal (23 states)	25,774	49.53	56.00	9,399	26.09	32.30	6.91
District of Columbia	77	78.8	85.6	30	31.2	34.3	17.78
Total	25,851	50.75	57.23	9,429	26.43	32.39	7.36

Data from Yerkes, 1921, and Statistical Abstract of the United States, 1902.

that by an enriched educational program the I.Q. of the group could be boosted 33 points. "There can be no doubt that moving children from an extremely deprived environment to good average environmental circumstances can boost the I.Q. some 20 to 30 points and in certain extreme cases as much as 60 or 70 points." (Jensen, 1969: 60)

Finally, what does the 15-point difference between whites' and blacks' I.Q. mean? First, many studies do not show the 15-point spread; some show as little as 10 points. The percentage differences range from 10 percent in New York to 83.36 percent in Florida based on the widely

FIGURE 6-4

Percentage Differences on Army Alpha Scores
(From Spuhler and Lindzey, 1967)

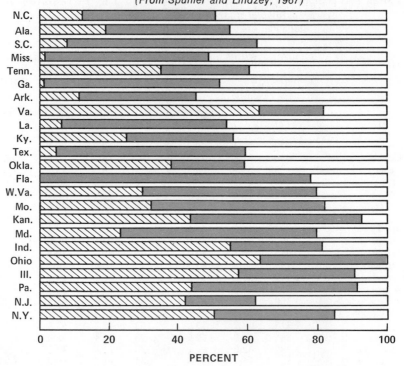

Percentage differences between Negro median Army Alpha scores in each of 23 states and lowest overall median score (cross hatching at left of each bar), between Negro and white median scores (shaded area in the middle), and between highest overall score and median white scores in the several states (at right of each bar). The states are listed from top to bottom in increasing rank of school expenditures per child of ages 5 to 18 during 1900. The length of the middle section of each bar (shaded area) is often taken to estimate the part of the variation due to genetic factors, and the lengths of the end sections the part due to environmental factors.

quoted Army Alpha Tests. The range of scores or the differences in I.Q. mean can be accounted for by environmental factors which will boost low I.Q. scores far more than any group differences. As Osborn (1971: 153) observed: "Differences in test intelligence between the major races are no greater than can be accounted for by the known differences in their environments."

There is a fatal flaw in the many arguments over I.Q. inheritance and environment: it is the assumption that a high heritability measured on one population means that environmental influence is small. It follows from such arguments then that any enrichment programs are wasted. Nothing could be further from the truth, as we have discussed. H^2 is not a measure of the magnitude of genetic contribution; a figure of 80 percent for H^2 *does not* mean that environment only influences 20 percent of the phenotypic expression. Many studies have shown how differences between population can be reduced drastically or erased entirely, and this is what we should be concerned with: the equalizing of environments and the increasing of educational opportunities.

RECOMMENDED READINGS AND LITERATURE CITED

ALLAND, ALEXANDER, JR. 1971. "Intelligence in black and white," in *Race and Intelligence*, C. L. Brace, G. R. Gamble, and J. T. Bond, eds., Anthropological Studies No. 8, American Anthropological Association, pp. 32–36.

CAVALLI-SFORZA, L. L., and BODMER, W. F. 1970. "Intelligence and race," *Scientific American*, 223(4): 19–29.

———. 1971. *The Genetics of Human Populations*. San Francisco: W. H. Freeman & Co.

GORDON, EDMUND W. 1969. "Discussion," in *Science and the Concept of Race*, Margaret Mead, Theodosius Dobzhansky, Ethel Tobach, and Robert E. Light, eds. New York: Columbia University Press, pp. 69–74.

GREEN, LELAND J. 1967. "Functional neurological performance in primitive cultures," *Human Potential*, 1 (1): 19–26.

GREGG, THOMAS G., and PEGGY R. SANDAY. 1971. "Genetic and environmental components of differential intelligence," in *Race and Intelligence, op. cit. supra*, pp. 58–63.

HARDIN, GARRETT. 1963. "A second sermon on the Mount," *Perspectives in Biology and Medicine*, 6(3): 366–371.

HIRSCH, JERRY. 1969. "Behavior-genetics, or 'Experimental,' analysis: The challenge of science versus the lure of technology," in *Behavioral Genetics: Methods and Research*, Martin Manosevitz, Gardner Lindzey, and Delbert D. Thiessen, ed. New York: Appleton-Century-Crofts, pp. 37–58.

JENSEN, ARTHUR R. 1969. "How much can we boost IQ and scholastic achievement?" in *Environment, Heredity, and Intelligence. Harvard Educational Review*, pp. 1-123.

———. 1971. "Can we and should we study race differences?" in *Race and Intelligence, op. cit. supra*, pp. 10–31.

OSBORN, FREDERICK. 1971. "Races and the future of man," in *The Biological and Social Meaning of Race*, Richard H. Osborne, ed. San Francisco: W. H. Freeman & Co., pp. 148–157.

PENROSE, L. S. 1951. "Measurement of pleiotrophic effects in phenylkelonuria," *Annals of Eugenics*, 16: 134–141.

PETTIGREW, THOMAS F. 1971. "Race, mental illness and intelligence: A social psychological view," in *The Biological and Social Meaning of Race, op. cit. supra,* pp. 87–124.

REED, T. EDWARD. 1969. "Caucasian genes in American Negroes," *Science,* 165: 762–768.

SCARR-SALAPATEK, SANDRA. 1971. "Race, social class and IQ," *Science,* 174: 1285–1295.

SCOTT, J. P. 1969. "Discussion," in *Science and the Concept of Race, op. cit. supra,* pp. 59–68.

SHOCKLEY, WM. 1972. "Dysgenics, geneticity, raceology: A challenge to the intellectual responsibility of educators," *Phi Delta Kappan,* 53(5): 297–307.

SPUHLER, JAMES N. and GARDNER LINDZEY. 1967. "Racial differences in behavior," in *Behavior-genetic Analysis,* Jerry Hirsch, ed. New York: McGraw-Hill.

STANTON, WM. R. 1960. *The Leopard's Spots: Scientific Attitudes Toward Race in America, 1815–59.* Chicago: University of Chicago Press.

chapter seven

The Future
of
The Human Species

By far the most important recent human evolutionary change is the radical alteration of birth and death rates throughout the world. (Crow, 1971: 309)

The question of human evolution has been raised many times in the past, and much of the preceding discussion involved a consideration of evolutionary processes. But why should the processes of interaction between man and environment occupy so much space in the writings on human biology during this past decade? One answer is that a study of evolution, as a total process, will enable man to discover the underlying causes of variations in modern populations. In this chapter we will summarize some of the interactions already considered and show how modern man, both in industrialized and primitive societies, has responded.

One measure of biologic success is the time required for a population to double its size (doubling time), and Table 7-1 shows that human population growth was very slow, hence the doubling time was quite long, until modern times. Until quite recently man, as a species, has not been spectacularly successful. From an estimated 5,000,000 people in 8000 B.C. a time when the agricultural revolution was becoming established, the population doubled on the average every 1,500 years until A.D. 1650. By then, almost 10,000 years later, *H. sapiens* had increased in numbers one hun-

TABLE 7-1

Doubling Time

(After Ehrlich and Holdren, 1973: 21)

Date	Estimated World Population	Doubling Time
8000 B.C	5,000,000	1,500 years
A.D. 1650	500,000,000	200 years
A.D. 1850	1,000,000,000	80 years
A.D. 1930	2,000,000,000	45 years
A.D. 1975	4,000,000,000	35 years

dred times, but it still required two hundred years (or eight generations) for a doubling to 1,000 million in A.D. 1850. Throughout many generations population growth was slow and not without setbacks, as shown in Figure 7-1. The species was growing at a rate of 0.2 percent per year in 1700, but periodic epidemics often severely cut back population size. The

FIGURE 7-1

**Growth in Numbers of Homo Sapiens and His Ancestors
Over the Past One-Half Million Years**

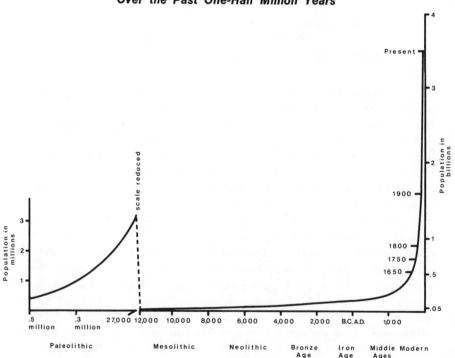

best-known event was the series of plague epidemics beginning in Europe in the fourteenth century. If growth rate is taken as a measure of success, then by 1970 man had become very successful indeed, and the species was growing by 2 percent per year (doubling time, 35 years). But until the past few hundred years man's position as a species was precarious.

Just what factors contributed to the accelerating growth rate in recent centuries is hard to determine. During the nineteenth century we can point to the control of infectious diseases as the main reason for declining death rates and hence population growth. In the seventeenth, eighteenth, and early nineteenth centuries, however, control of disease was probably not the single most important reason for growth. It is likely that increased efficiency in food production was more important. By this period population pressures had reached the point where many millions migrated to new lands; the colonial expansion by western Europeans is an example. Yet, while these technologically advanced societies were seeking new space, many, perhaps most, of the world's population were living at pre-seventeenth-century technological levels. Many African and New World peoples were less numerous in proportion to the carrying capacity of their lands then were Asians and Europeans.

With this rapid expansion the modern era was begun and the conditions under which man lives today were initiated. These modern living conditions, though complex, have capacity to change rapidly; and as conditions or environments change, selective forces are altered readily. Natural selection in a previous period that favored one group over another is changed, and a major result is a shift in population size and reproduction rate, which will alter the population growth rate. However, all populations of *H. sapiens* are not affected equally, nor is the selective pressure in effect everywhere at the same time.

Bushmen, who today occupy Africa's Kalahari Desert, were probably as numerous as Europeans 10,000 years ago. The Europeans have expanded and successfully occupied new areas of the world, while the Bushmen, who number only a few thousand, have been pushed into a harsh refuge area by expanding prehistoric agriculturalists, such as the Bantu-speaking peoples and more recently the Europeans (see Hulse, 1955). The end result of a disproportionate increase of the world's peoples is a distribution that often differs radically from that of prehistoric times. The future, if growth projections are reasonably accurate, is a further change in the distribution of the world's peoples (see Figure 7-2). Those countries with greater natural and technological resources have a slower projected growth rate than the less developed areas of the world (see Figure 7-3).

The major differences in growth are due to a dramatic lowering of the death rate. Where both birth and death rates were high, a reduction

FIGURE 7-2

Shift in Population Proportions

(From Frejka, 1973)

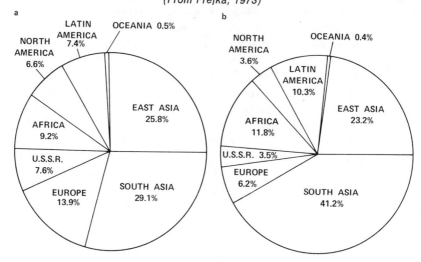

Shift in proportions of the population living in eight major areas of the world is portrayed as it could be expected under projection 4, which assumes a net reproduction rate of 1 by the period 2020 to 2025. The present proportions (a) are compared with the projected proportions for the year 2100 (b). The eight areas are employed by the United Nations for socioeconomic classification.

in only the death rate would, of course, result in rapid population growth, as experienced by Africa, Asia, and Latin America in the past few decades. The effects that these growth phenomena have on evolution depend a great deal on how one views the population structure, its mating circles, social systems, and age structure. Some investigators feel that, since death rates are low, selection operates through a variation in birth rates. This is effected mostly through a voluntary decision of the parents, made according to the dictates of their culture or society, often with consideration of the advantage to the family. One writer expressed the situation in this way: "Selection is for reproductive success, and in man reproductive success is primarily determined by the social system and by culture. Effective behavior is the question, not something else." (Washburn, 1964: 243)

With the reduction of death rates and the concomitant rise in population, much concern has been expressed over what was thought to be the decline of the species. Interest in the advantages of controlled breeding of man, or *eugenics,* was developed in the late nineteenth century by Galton in England. It was believed that through a "science" of selective

FIGURE 7-3
Regional Growth, 1650–1970
(From Frejka, 1973)

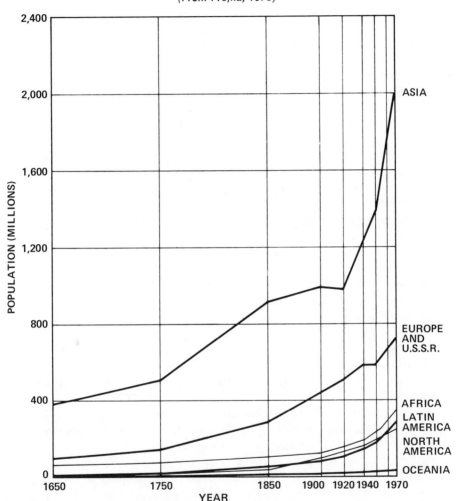

Regional growth of the world's population from 1650 to 1970 is
portrayed. At the beginning of the period the total population
of the world was about 553 million. By 1850 it was 1.3 billion.
Since 1900 it has gone from 1.6 billion to the present 3.6 billion.

human breeding the effects of the reduction of natural selection in modern
society, which was believed to cause species decline, could be reversed.
The belief was then held, and is still held by many today, that our species
was complete and that evolution has ceased, no further changes being

possible. But the truth is otherwise. Populations grow or decline, gene frequencies alter, and natural selection—that is, differential reproduction —still operates. True, the environmental forces are filtered through the protective or isolating layer of man's culture, and social factors such as assortative mating play a stronger role in the reduction of natural selection. *H. sapiens* gene combinations, however, are still altering, at least in part from natural selection, particularly in those groups with the most rapid growth rates, those in the underdeveloped countries.

Evidence for the evolution of modern man is difficult to identify and obtain, and there are no examples comparable to those found among insects or other simpler organisms with short lifespans. But evidence of an indirect sort exists if we compare modern man living under civilized conditions in highly industrialized societies with peoples living under conditions comparable to those which existed several thousands of years ago. Life expectancy is lower at all ages in primitive societies, and fewer individuals live into their sixteenth year.

Comparisons of skeletal remains of modern and prehistoric peoples show that fewer developmental anomalies occur among prehistoric remains than in modern civilized populations. Often pathological lesions are fewer, particularly among primitives, who live by hunting and gathering. Even with prehistoric materials a contrast is seen; those more ancient populations who depended on hunting for subsistence were more "healthy" or normal than were the early agriculturalists. Developmental anomalies in the form of missing or misplaced teeth, poorly formed palates, and improper cranial suture closure abound in remains from primitive agriculturalists; such conditions are seen less frequently among the remains from nonagricultural groups, even those populations from the same period.

Several other characteristics are worth investigating, particularly those that relate to pregnancy, birth, and infant mortality. An example is the evidence that insufficiency of breast milk in newly delivered mothers, is, at least in part, genetically based. There is a higher frequency of this deficiency in populations who have had the longest history of possessing dairy animals. Infant mortality rates are generally higher and birth rates lower in wandering primitive hunting groups; hence a stronger, more intense selection exists than in sedentary agricultural groups. But many other factors related to diet and disease may cause differentiation among populations of various cultural forms.

Since man has spent approximately 99 percent of his time as a species sustaining himself by his hunting and foraging activities, we should take note of these contrasts. The greater number of skeletal defects, the higher frequency of color blindness and visual deficiency among peoples whose ancestors had been sedentary agriculturalists the longest is explained by the argument that this "new" mode of life for *H. sapiens* reduced many of the stringent selective forces that acted during the hunting and gathering phase of our evolution. This relaxation of selection adds to the numbers of defects present in each generation, however these defects are determined. The frequency of the polygenic characters described above or the increase in the frequency of genes that interrupt certain metabolic pathways, such as the recessive genes that prevent synthesis of melanin in an albino or the gene that blocks the formation of the enzyme that metabolizes galactose (see page 87), may be used as evidence for relaxed selection.

The accumulation of defective genes increases the overall genetic load (defined as the frequency of detrimental genes which are usually recessives but sometimes dominants). In recent times the wider application of improved medical treatment has maintained many who would have perished for the lack of care in former times. The improvement in prenatal care and treatment at birth have greatly reduced infant deaths, and many with congenital or genetically based defects are able to survive. But this increase of the so-called load on our species is not all negative and, because it increases species diversity, may have a very positive survival value over a period of many generations.

Finally, technology considered in balance, even though it provides for population increase, also has some negative effects. Some can be seen in primitive agriculturalists, whose sedentary life brought larger groups of people into prolonged contact with one another, enhancing the spread of cholera, smallpox, plague, and other diseases. Later the rise of city-states further accelerated the processes of introducing man to new disease forms; also, a narrowing of the dietary base reduced the chance that all necessary nutrients would be acquired. The building of irrigation canals in modern times opened more lands for agriculture to feed an ever larger population, but in many parts of the world this network of waterways spreads a snail-borne parasite which causes a severe ailment—Bilharziasias. Roads built to open new lands to exploitation increase population mobility and accelerate the spread of many diseases caused by parasitic organisms. Today's cities create an entirely new environment with noise, pollution, and many other phenomena unknown to prehistoric man. In the modern urban environment the primitive hunter with his perfect 20/20 eyes, well-formed nasal septum, and color vision would have no advantage over modern populations who, with an allotment of defective genes, maintain life in ever-growing numbers.

The growth of population, its redistribution, and the decline of disease over the last few centuries have had far-reaching effects on the range and composition of *H. sapiens'* variation. Adaptations to life both before and after the industrial revolution have placed a great burden on the species with the rise of population density, change in dwelling space, increase in disease transmission, and intensified psychological stress. The course of evolution and the future distribution of human variation perhaps is difficult to explain or predict, but it can at least be described in some of the ways discussed in the balance of this chapter.

MORTALITY RATES
AND POPULATION GROWTH

Everywhere today the death rate is low, as shown by Table 7-2. These data from selected countries show that deaths are less than half of birth rates, which means a net annual increase in most cases of from 0.5 to 3 percent. The higher rates occur invariably in the underdeveloped countries, where population doubling times are approximately one generation. Population projections for the next decade provide estimates of 20 percent increase worldwide—10 percent increase in industrialized countries and 25 percent increase in the underdeveloped. The world will likely contain 4,933 million people by 1985 if present trends continue, which is an increase from 3,782 million in 1972. This increase will not be evenly distributed, and major shifts in population centers will place a heavier burden on limited resources in the areas of the world which experience the heaviest increases.

Infant Mortality

This phenomenal population growth is due mainly to lower infant death rates, which everywhere have been drastically reduced. In the United States today, 95 percent of all children born alive reach their thirteenth birthday, compared to only 50 percent one hundred years ago. Table 7-3 shows comparative data on infant mortality for selected countries. Group one countries have death rates of less than 20 per 1,000 live births, whereas those in group three have rates as high as 92 per 1,000. All countries listed in this table have experienced a dramatic reduction of death rates over the past 70 years; India, from a high of 200 per 1,000 in 1898 to 40 per 1,000 in 1972, is the most striking. Today, India is one of the world regions that is growing most rapidly, 2.5 percent per annum, which provides a projected population size in 1985 of 807 million.

While infant mortality has declined during the last few generations from 50 percent to between 5 and 10 percent, the maternal death rate has also declined from 320 per 100,000 to 22 per 100,000. These striking reductions, made possible by a combination of improved diet and increased maternal care, have radically altered the selective forces acting

TABLE 7-2

Rate of Increase, Birth and Death Rates, Area and Density for the World, Major Areas and Regions: Selected Years

(Modified from Demographic Yearbook 1968 and 1972)

Major Areas	Estimates of midyear population (millions)				Annual rate of pop. increase 1965-72	Birth rate per 1000 pop. 1965-72	Death rate per 1000 pop. 1965-72	No. of yrs. dbl. from 1972	Area	Density
	1930	1950	1968	1972						
Africa	164	222	336	364	2.6	47	21	27	30320	12
Western Africa	48	67	106	107	2.5	49	24	28	6142	17
Eastern Africa	46	63	93	103	2.6	47	22	27	6338	16
Northern Africa	39	53	81	92	3.1	47	17	23	8525	11
Middle Africa	21	25	34	38	2.2	45	24	32	6613	6
Southern Africa	10	14	22	24	2.4	41	17	29	2701	9
Asia	1120	1381	1946	2154	2.3	38	15	30	27655	78
East Asia	591	684	889	962	1.8	32	14	39	11757	82
S. W., Middle South & S. E. Asia	529	697	1057	1191	2.8	44	17	25	15898	75
Oceania	10.0	12.7	18.5	20.2	2.1	25	10	33	8510	2

TABLE 7-2 (Continued)

Rate of Increase, Birth and Death Rates, Area and Density for the World, Major Areas and Regions: Selected Years

(Modified from Demographic Yearbook 1968 and 1972)

Major Areas	Estimates of midyear population (millions)				Annual rate of pop. increase 1965-72	Birth rate per 1000 pop. 1965-72	Death rate per 1000 pop. 1965-72	No. of yrs. dbl. from 1972	Area	Density
	1930	1950	1968	1972						
America	242	329	489	533	2.1	29	10	33	42083	13
Northern America	134	166	222	233	1.2	18	9	58	21515	11
Latin America	108	163	267	300	2.9	38	10	24	20567	15
Tropical South America	55	84	142	160	3.0	40	10	23	13700	12
Middle America	22	35	63	72	3.4	44	10	20	2496	29
Temperate South America	19	27	38	41	1.8	26	9	39	4134	10
Caribbean	12	17	24	27	2.2	35	11	32	238	113
USSR – URSS	179	180	238	248	1.0	18	8	70	22402	11
Europe	355	392	455	469	0.8	17	10	87	4936	95
Western Europe	108	123	147	151	0.7	16	11	100	995	151
Southern Europe	93	108	126	131	0.9	19	9	78	1315	99
Eastern Europe	89	88	102	106	0.8	17	10	87	990	107
Northern Europe	65	73	80	82	0.6	17	11	117	1636	50

TABLE 7-3

Average Infant Mortality Per 1,000 Live Births [1]

Country	1898-1902	1918-1922	1956-1960	1972
Sweden	98	65	17	11.7
Japan	155	172	36	13
Norway	88	–	20	13.8
Denmark	131	84	24	14.8
France	154	112	32	15.1
England and Wales	152	85	23	18.4
United States	162	85	26	19.2
U.S.S.R.	–	–	81	24.4
Spain	190	158	49	27.9
Italy	167	141	47	29.2
India	200	212	98	42
Argentina	–	–	61	58
Mexico	–	–	76	69
Guatemala	–	–	95	92

[1] Based on various sources.

on our species. The chief result has been to reduce the selection that has acted against those genetic anomalies that result in early death or that may cause susceptibility to a variety of ailments to which infants are normally subjected. Declining maternal mortality has effectively increased overall fertility and is one of the major causes of the growth rates shown in Table 7-2.

In addition to the variation in mortality-rate reduction between world areas, there are significant differences between social classes (see Table 7-4). These differences have caused shifts in population percentages of various classes in the past three generations and are likely to continue. Alteration in fertility and growth rates among socioeconomic classes and ethnic groups within any country are much more difficult to define or to predict. Statuses often shift easily, and fashions change as preferences for large or small families alter. The immediate result is wide fluctuation in group size and proportion, as observed by Osborn (1971: 370–371):

The first result of the reduction in births was greatly to increase differential fertility between social, economic and educational groups. . . . The great post-war baby boom was largely a phenomenon of the white-collar classes. Their birth rate almost doubled between 1940 and 1960 and accounted for most of the rise in births in that period. The proportion of families of five or more children continued its long decline. Group differentials lost much of their significance.

TABLE 7-4

Causes of Death by Color and Sex in United States for 1955–1968, Rates Per 100,000 Population [1]

	Total 1955	Total 1968	White—1955		Nonwhite—1955		White—1968		Nonwhite—1968	
			Males	Females	Males	Females	Males	Females	Males	Females
Diseases of heart	355.8	372.6	437.9	292.4	317.6	255.8	451.4	319.2	327.1	258.9
Malignant neoplasms	146.5	159.4	160.1	141.0	119.8	108.5	180.8	145.6	157.7	113.4
Vascular lesions of central nervous system	106.0	105.8	102.3	106.2	117.8	112.9	97.4	112.0	111.5	112.8
Influenza and pneumonia	27.1	36.8	27.8	21.3	57.5	40.1	39.1	31.1	59.6	39.7
Arteriosclerosis	19.8	16.8	20.5	20.7	14.2	11.7	–	19.7	–	10.1
Diabetes mellitus	15.5	19.2	12.8	18.5	9.7	18.6	16.0	21.0	17.3	30.0
Tuberculosis	9.1	–	11.2	4.1	28.4	15.0	–	–	–	–
Infant mortality per 1000 live births	26.4	21.8	23.6		42.8		19.2		34.5	

[1] Based on various sources.

Major Causes of Death

Causes of death have undergone significant alteration during this century see Table 7-5). Several diseases, once major causes of death, no longer add to the overall mortality. The incidences of typhoid, communicable diseases of childhood, tuberculosis, and pneumonia, once responsible for high death rates, have declined to insignificant levels. Cardiovascular diseases and cancer have steadily increased to become number one killers. Several kinds of respiratory diseases had also increased to significant levels by 1970, taking about 15 lives per 100,000 population. Chronic bronchitis is on the increase, possibly because of the rise in air pollution, and is becoming a major cause of disability in the world, ranking with heart disease as a cause of death in England.

The leading causes of death are not always the same throughout the world. The three leading causes of death in industrialized countries are heart disease, cancer, and vascular lesions, in contrast to gastroenteritis, pneumonia, and malaria for many underdeveloped countries. Even allowing for poor records and errors in diagnosis where medical services are primitive, these disease incidences are interesting contrasts and point to significant differences in the selective forces to which these populations are subjected.

TABLE 7-5

Average Annual Death Rates Per 100,000 From Selected Causes, United States, 1900–1970 [1]

Cause of Death	1900–04	1920–24	1940–44	1955	1970
All causes	1622.3	1198.0	1062.0	930.4	
Cardiovascular-renal diseases	359.2	369.4	390.3	506.0	501
Cancer	67.6	86.8	123.1	146.5	162
Accidents, all forms	79.1	70.6	73.0	56.9	54.2
Bronchitis, emphysema, and asthma					14.9
Diabetes mellitus	12.2	18.3	26.5	15.5	18.5
Cirrhosis of liver	13.0	7.4	8.6	10.2	15.8
Tuberculosis	184.8	97.1	43.4	9.1	2.7
Pneumonia and influenza	184.4	141.1	63.7	27.1	30.5
Diarrhea and enteritis	115.6	43.2	9.8	4.7	1.1
Communicable diseases of childhood	65.3	34.0	4.6	0.7	0.1
Typhoid fever	26.8	7.4	0.6	–	–
Syphilis	12.9	17.5	12.6	2.3	0.2
Appendicitis	9.3	14.0	7.3	1.4	0.7
Infant mortality	–	77.1	42.6	26.4	20.9

[1] Based on various sources.

DISEASE EPIDEMICS AND SELECTION

There is a high probability that a majority of our genetic polymorphisms are the result of former selection for resistance to certain
diseases in the past. The high incidence of typhus, plague, cholera, and
smallpox, to mention a few major epidemic diseases often experienced
by mankind, eliminated many thousands of persons, leaving only those
who were able to withstand them. Typhoid, for instance, killed almost
as many men in the Union Army during the Civil War as died on the
field of battle—81,000 versus 93,000. Typhus, a scourge of the military
for thousands of years, reduced Napoleon's armies by one-fifth in 1813.
Smallpox, known for centuries, is one of the deadliest of the epidemic
diseases, claiming four out of ten victims. This disease has raged un-
checked through populations who lacked a history of contact with the
disease. An estimated three and one-half million Indians died in Mexico
after Cortez's invasion, greatly facilitating the Spanish conquest.

Periodic outbreaks of smallpox occur even in populations with a
long history of the disease. In 1770, 3,000,000 died in India and another
500,000 in 1873. The disease has been so feared that even in modern
times minor outbreaks of a few cases in industrialized countries send
health authorities into a panic, and stringent regulations are generally
enforced.

Cholera, once a major cause of epidemics, has also been practically
eliminated except in a few areas. Some 50,000 deaths were reported
in New York in 1866, but only a handful in 1900, while 800,000 cholera
deaths were recorded in India in that year. This disease, though controlled now in modern societies, breaks out periodically in Africa and
India, and the World Health Organization reports that it is on the
increase again, with a total case load of about 70,000 including 21,000
deaths recorded in 1965.

During those recent times when bacterial and protozoan diseases
were at their peak, any gene or gene combination that reduced susceptibility would have a marked effect on survival. The selective advantage
of certain genotypes in an era of massive epidemics would have been an
important factor in the biological evolution of man, particularly in recent times with rapid growth rates and major population shifts. The most
recent major outbreaks, summarized in Table 7-6, can be used to trace a
significant change in man's disease environment. The total effect has been
the alteration of combinations of disease organisms with which man is in
most frequent contact.

These changing patterns of disease and mortality undoubtedly
cause alteration in gene frequencies, and certain polymorphisms will

be selected for or against in the future. Examination of disease influences can provide a way of interpreting population variation and selection through time. Anthropologists attempting to understand human diversity several generations in the future will likely be puzzled by the persistence

TABLE 7-6

Historical Outline of Three Selected Diseases [1]

Disease	Date	Epidemic History	Deaths Reported
Plague	540	Beginning of first Pandemic, which lasted 50 to 60 years in Europe	100,000,000 (estimated)
	1338	Start of second Pandemic, which lasted nearly three centuries	25–43,000,000
	1664	Last outbreak of plague of the second Pandemic in London	
	1855	Start of third Pandemic, which covered a greater land area, including the U.S., India, China, and Mongolia, which suffered the worst	13,000,000 (mostly 1896–1917)
	1907	Year of maximum death rate of third Pandemic	1,315,892
	1923	Third Pandemic	250,000
	1942	Last outbreak of third Pandemic	10,577
Smallpox	15–17th centuries	American Indian populations	Millions of deaths estimated
	17th century	Outbreak in Europe	60,000,000
	1707	Iceland	18,000 of total population of 50,000
	1721	Boston's sixth epidemic—5,985 with disease	895
	1770	India	3,000,000
	1776	Almost half of Revolutionary army of 10,000 suffered from the disease	
	1873	India	500,000
	1870	France, time of Franco-Prussian War, 100,000 cases	25,000
	1885	Montreal, Canada, 20,000 cases	3,000
	1921	U.S., 89,357 cases	481
	1945	U.S., 346 cases	12
	1950	U.S., 42 cases	None
Cholera	1817	With India as a focal point, disease spread to Ceylon, Java, Borneo, and Indonesia	100,000 (reported in Java)
	1831	Mecca	18,000 (in 3 weeks)
	1832	England	5,432
	1832	Belgium	8,000
	1832	Canada—disease spread through U.S. to Mexico, Peru, and Chile	1,000 (in 2 weeks)
	1866	The fourth Pandemic dates from this year with a major outbreak in Russia	90,000

TABLE 7-6 *(Continued)*

Historical Outline of Three Selected Diseases [1]

Disease	Date	Epidemic History	Deaths Reported
	1866	U.S.	50,000
	1867	Sardinia	130,000
	1875	Hungary	190,000
	1877	China	89,000 (estimated)
	1899	Start of sixth Pandemic, which lasted until 1923	
	1900	Worst year of cholera on record, a major outbreak in India	800,000
	1906	India	682,649
	1919	India	565,166
	1960–1970	Today a total world case load of 70,000 per year	21,000 (estimated)

[1] Based on Gallagher, 1969, and Stamp, 1964.

of many seemingly deleterious genes—unless, of course, they understand man's history and take into account the alteration of environmental factors and natural selection.

GENETIC LOAD
AND REDUCED SELECTION

With changing environments and reduction of the stringent selection exerted by epidemic diseases, chronic ailments are on the rise, as shown by the death rates listed in the accompanying tables. Additionally, as society provides improved care of afflicted individuals, the genetic load of the population increases. This simply means that congenital defects or genetic propensities toward a disease have less and less effect on fitness of individuals, because medical treatment reduces the selective disadvantage which existed in prior times. Overall, the pattern of survival changes as life styles are altered, as disease environments are controlled, and as medical maintenance increases.

Relaxed selection has the apparent effect of increasing the frequency of defective phenotypes in a population. Impressive evidence along these lines has turned up in studies of the frequency of color blindness among primitive and industrialized societies. Australian Aborigine males have a rate of 2 percent while Chinese and Japanese populations have between 4 and 7 percent, which contrasts with the 5 to 10 percent of European and Western Asian populations studied. The argument is that our preagricultural ancestors had a low frequency of this visual defect, which presumably would have been a handicap in their hunting activities. Those populations furthest removed in time from the hunting past would have a larger number of color-vision defectives, just as these studies have demonstrated. Visual acuity, in general, is better among "primitives" tested than among "civilized" populations, particularly in the case of myopia. There are fewer nearsighted individuals among hunters and gatherers today; also, many more people with better than 20/20 vision are found. We can appreciate the obvious advantage when we consider the rigors of hunters' life styles and their reliance on foraging activities.

The time depth of such investigations is obviously limited; the subjects studied can only span a few generations. Defects in the formation of the skeletal or dental structures, however, can be compared over thousands of generations. One such study reported the significant increase of deformed nasal septums among skeletal remains of recent and modern populations over earlier groups. The modern skeleton had appreciably higher frequencies of developmental defects in the nasal septal region; several of these defects were the kind that would have impaired breathing. Other deviations such as persistence of the metopic suture (suture which divides the frontal bone until at the end of the first year when it fuses) into adulthood, the occurrence of "peg-shaped" teeth, the lack of a third molar (agenesis), and malformed palates all show up with greater frequency in modern man, though the range is great. Only 5 percent of some primitives show malocclusion, while as many as 82 percent of American children do. There is also a significant difference between primitive agriculturalists and hunters and gatherers, the greatest number of defective bone and tooth formations being found in the agriculturalists, as discussed earlier.

These traits, or developmental defects, are probably polygenic and are subject to wide variation in their expression. It is difficult to demonstrate which selective force or forces are actively working to favor certain phenotypes, but the preliminary evidence does show a developmental quality distinction between populations at different time and cultural levels. Presumptive evidence is then provided of accumulated effects of relaxed selection over time. After the Neolithic period, judging from the skeletal record, selection has been reduced, permitting many structural variants to appear with increased frequency. Reduced face and tooth sizes, skeletal defects, and missing or extra teeth are a few of these features.

In recent times among industrialized societies, many hereditary disorders that affect the potential survival of infants have been corrected. Cleft palate, which occurs about once in 2,500 births and often resulted in death in earlier times, has been correctable by surgery for many years. Before 1912 infants born with a minor muscular defect of the pyloric sphincter of the stomach, which prevented food from passing into the small intestine, died. This far from rare defect (2–4/1,000), is easily corrected by surgery, which enables normal digestive function.

Before the 1920's diabetes often resulted in death, but the development of insulin treatment has made it possible to maintain diabetics and to enable them to lead a relatively normal life under the proper care and treatment. The affliction is believed to have an underlying genetic factor, since some individuals seem to have a greater propensity for it. It is more frequent in women than in men and in general is strikingly higher in certain ethnic groups; Papago Indians of the Southwest and Polynesians have a high rate of diabetes. In the United States population there were 600,000 diabetics in 1945, and the disease apparently was on the increase three decades later with over two million reported. Whether this rise is due to an increase in the frequency of defective genes in the population or to a change in life style is hard to say; probably both factors are involved.

Ethnic group differences in the incidence of several diseases have long been reported. Table 7-7 lists a few groups, some defects which may have genetic basis, their relative frequencies and several disorders inherited by simple genetic factors. These relative frequencies are the result of both population size and inbreeding as well as of the population's history of selective factors. In the case of clubfoot (probably caused by a partially penetrant dominant) among Hawaiians, with 68 affected individuals per 10,000 live births, the cause is probably tied in with the small size of the original founding population, some of whom probably carried the defective gene. In Caucasians generally the frequency is below 11/10,000, and it is 6/10,000 among people of oriental ancestry. Congenital malformations of the hip joint, which may be genetically determined, also occur with greater frequency in certain ethnic groups: 1.3/1,000 live births in American whites contrasted to 10.9/1,000 among Navaho Indians. The reasons for these differences are not known, nor are the evolutionary implications, if any, understood.

Several simply inherited disorders are now known, and a few have been subjected to rather elaborate investigations in the last few years. One is PKU, a severe metabolic defect described on page 85. With proper treatment the affected person can develop normally, which will probably increase the frequency of the recessive gene within our population, thereby adding to the overall genetic load of mutants. Hemophilia afflicts one out of 25,000 males, and with increasing improvement in medical treatment the 17-year life expectancy should be extended. Cystic fibrosis, probably also caused by a recessive, is now manageable,

TABLE 7-7

Ethnic Groups and Disease Incidence

(Modified from Damon, 1962, 1971; McKusick, 1962, and various sources)

Ethnic Groups	Relatively High Prevalence of these disorders
African Black	Abnormal Hemoglobin Hb^S, Hb^C, Thalassemia G6PD deficiency (African type) Hypertension Polydactyly Cervical Cancer Sarcoidosis
American Indians Papago Apache	 Diabetes mellitus Congenital hip dislocation
Ashkenazic Jews	Tay-Sachs disease Pentosuria Stub fingers Bloom's disease Leukemia Diabetes Mellitus
Chinese	Thalassemia G6PD deficiency (Chinese type) Nasopharyngeal cancer
Europeans Northern Southern	 Phenylketonuria Pernicious anemia Cleft Palate G6PD deficiency (Mediterranean type) Thalassemia
Japanese	Acatalasia Oguchi's disease Cleft lip - palate Gastric cancer

and some patients are now reaching adolescence. These characteristics, and many more identified as due to defective genes in modern populations, may not prove the approach of a "genetic plague" predicted by some, but at least the higher survival potential of persons with defective genotypes forecasts an increase in the genetic load of our species, measured in numbers of lethal mutants or of genetic polymorphisms which in former times would have reduced overall fitness. Experiments with chromosome structures and cell cultures hold the promise that a form of "genetic" engineering in the future will be able to correct the defective gene.

Selective Breeding

With the rise of the genetic load of *H. sapiens* a logical course might seem to be regulation and control of mating in order to attempt to counteract the increase in detrimental mutants. It is fairly obvious that persons who carry a dominant gene which results in some defective development like achondrodystrophy, retinoblastoma, or vitamin-D resistant rickets should carefully consider before producing children, but the case of recessive genes of low frequency is somewhat different. The chance that two persons who carry the same recessive alleles will mate is fairly remote, except in the case of cousins or individuals from the same small endogamous populations. In such cases, professional genetic counseling would alert the potential mates to the possibilities of producing defective offspring. The absolute control of human breeding and/or the use of sperm banks as advocated in the past is another matter. The full or even partial application of eugenics methods leaves much to be desired because of many unanswered questions. One of these is the probable higher fitness of the heterozygote; another is simply what trait is to be selected for, which is a serious consideration since our species has survived and evolved through millenia because of our genetic variability. Given this, some or most of our genetic load may be desirable, since it adds to our heterzygosity.

The increased human control of the environment and the ability to find ways of ameliorating inherited defects has reduced the need for selective breeding or eugenics. Man owes his success as a species to cultural or exogenetic factors in addition to genetic adaptations. It is not the single gene in relation to the environment that determines fitness. The total fitness of an individual or a population is not measured by single or even groups of genotypes; it is the end result of the sum total of all genotypic interactions or, rather, the total genome.

Selective breeding for occupational aptitudes or for certain life styles or environments apparently has been a complete failure. The massive selective breeding program carried on in India for a hundred generations through its caste system has not produced classes genetically endowed to carry out certain types of jobs. The individual differences within each caste in India, or elsewhere where selection or endogamous breeding has taken place, have often shown as great a variety within each class as the differences that exist between them.

Man is a species whose genetic adaptations are to life styles of a distinct evolutionary past, mostly to a pre-agricultural, paleolithic form of life when population density was low and man was constantly on the move. This was the life style of our species until approximately 12,000 years ago, when a substantial number of *H. sapiens* became sedentary and adopted an agricultural technology. At that time nature began to select for new forms, aided by increases in certain diseases, alteration in mating circles, and an increase in population sizes. Gradually, through the millenia, we have altered our gene frequencies; as our environments are still changing, so will the frequencies of several genes continue to alter. However, with an elaboration of cultural technologies we are capable of altering environments within a time span much shorter than a human generation. This factor introduces a new element into human evolution; the rapid change in selective forces which places a heavy burden on our social systems and culture. Evolution, though, is still occurring in our species, and "ongoing evolution" is a reality.

ONGOING EVOLUTION
AND MAN OF THE FUTURE

The change in dwelling space, increased potential for disease transmission, and intensified psychological stresses of twentieth-century Society all contribute to ongoing evolution of modern *H. sapiens*. Natural selection today apparently operates most stringently on the urban dweller, subjected to noise, crowding, and foul air. These conditions place a burden on our neuroendocrine system, often stretching our psychological balance to the breaking point. The high mental-illness rate (one fourth of all hospital admissions), the increased use of mood-altering drugs, and the rise of stress-related diseases are all part of the cost of urban living. The cost of air pollution is illustrated by current respiratory diseases, notably bronchitis and emphysema, which have shown a steady increase in the last 25 years.

Air contamination may be a leading contributor to death among urban populations. Increased deaths are recorded during periods of particularly heavy pollution in cities, as graphically illustrated by Table 7-8. Whether these forms of environmental stresses will affect gene frequency of future generations remains to be demonstrated. However, there is one possible link that suggests a relationship between certain genotypes and air pollution. It appears that persons with emphysema have deficient quantities of alpha 1 anti-trypsin, a substance which inactivates trypsin and prevents this enzyme from splitting proteins except under the special conditions in the digestive tract. Emphysema patients possibly have too little of this inhibitor, and trypsin is probably at work partially digesting the fine membranes in the alveoli (air sacs) of the lungs. The lungs then lose

TABLE 7-8

Registered Deaths in London Administrative County by Age: Comparison of 7-Day Period before the 1952 Episode with the 7-Day Period that Included the Episode of Air Pollution

(From Dubos, 1968)

Age	7-Day Period Preceding the Episode	7-Day Period Including the Episode
Under 4 weeks	16	28
4 weeks to 1 year	12	26
1 – 14 years	10	13
15 – 44 years	61	99
45 – 64 years	237	652
65 – 74 years	254	717
75 years and over	355	949

elasticity, which is one of the typical symptoms of a major type of emphysema. It is believed that alpha 1 anti-trypsin deficiency is due to a single gene, and homozygotes or heterozygotes for this allele would probably be more susceptible to air pollution. This explanation is at present only a speculation, but it offers an example of how selective forces might be acting in urban environments.

Modern man's mobility is probably another major factor contributing to gene-frequency changes today. Increasingly, man is becoming more urban, and mating circles are ever widening. A few generations ago matings most always took place between persons within a limited geographic area; usually their childhood residences had been within a few hundred yards of each other. In much of the world this remains the case; village, class, or caste endogamy still is maintained. But as industrialization continues to spread throughout the world, our habits and customs break down and important alterations occur in mating circles. Gene exchange takes place over ever widening areas. In nineteenth-century England the bicycle increased the mean distance between prenuptial residences (see page 101), and in this century the automobile has had an even more significant influence on extending population boundaries.

This mobility and expansion of mating circles increases heterozygosity of the human species and decreases the chance of producing homozygous recessives. However, it increases the influence of assortative mating, particularly the preference for mating within one's own socioeconomic group or at the same educational level.

Another major factor in modern man's evolution is the reduced maternal mortality rate and the overall extension of female reproductive years. Last century the average age at menarche was 18 but today, in many countries, it is between 12 and 13. A later onset of menopause is usual today and has increased from age 44, the average a century ago to age 50. In modern industrialized societies the female reproductive span has been extended from 27 to 36 years. Though contraceptives reduce fecundity, the increased reproductive span and lower mortality rates are a major contribution to the rise in fertility, particularly in underdeveloped countries.

All of these factors—the shift in selective forces, population mobility, increased reproductive span, and entirely new disease stresses—contribute to ongoing evolution of modern *H. sapiens*. What the future holds is hard to say, but evidence is accumulating and more is being learned about the genetic basis for man's physiological response to the environment. Human variation exists now as it has in the past, though the boundaries, as defined, keep shifting and "ethnic" groups arise and disappear. Whether man will remain as diverse in the future, a few hundred generations hence, is not possible to predict. But we do know that our species is capable of numerous responses to environmental stresses, both by individual homostatic adjustments in the short term and genetic combination changes in the population in the long term.

We need to expand our research on human variation, but what is more important, we need to change our attitude and perspective. We need to appreciate human diversity for what it is—the result of a species gene pool responding to the stresses of natural selection as modified by man's behavior or culture. However, it is not a simple matter of explaining all diversity by the action of natural selection. Other factors are involved and should be taken into account, such as the breeding-population size, the social system, and the population's history.

Several kinds of variation have been discussed throughout this book, and again the author must apologize for the paucity of data. In many respects we know more about the surface of the moon than about *H. sapiens*' diversity. Extensive comparative studies must be made; the contrasts should be drawn between members of breeding populations; and use of large, all-encompassing taxons should be avoided. The challenges are there, the frontiers broad: students must rise to meet these challenges with their questions.

RECOMMENDED READINGS AND LITERATURE CITED

BRIERLEY, JOHN. 1970. *A Natural History of Man*. Cranbury, N.J.: Fairleigh Dickinson University Press.

BROWN, HARRISON. 1967. *The Challenge of Man's Future*. New York: The Viking Press.

CROW, JAMES F. 1971. "The quality of people: Human evolutionary changes," in *Natural Selection in Human Population,* Carl J. Bajema, ed. New York: John Wiley & Sons, pp. 309–320.

DAMON, ALBERT. 1971. "Race, ethnic group and disease," *Soc. Biol.,* 16: 69–80.

Demographic Yearbook, United Nations, 1968.

DUBOS, RENE. 1968. *Man Adapting.* New Haven: Yale University Press.

EHRLICH, PAUL R., ANNE H. EHRLICH, and JOHN P. HOLDREN. 1973. *Human Ecology.* San Francisco: W. H. Freeman & Co.

FREJKA, THOMAS. 1973. "The prospects for a stationary world population," *Scientific American,* 228(3): 15–23.

GALLAGHER, RICHARD. 1969. *Diseases that Plague Modern Man, a History of Ten Communicable Diseases.* Dobbs Ferry, N.Y.: Oceana Publications.

HEIMANN, H. 1961. "Effects of air pollution on human health," in *Air Pollution.* Geneva: World Health Organization Series, no. 46, pp. 159–220.

HULSE, FREDERICK S. 1955. "Technological advance and major racial stocks," *Human Biology,* 27: 184–192.

OSBORN, FREDERICK. 1971. "A return to the principles of natural selection," in *Natural Selection in Human Populations, op. cit. supra,* pp. 369–377.

SMITH, THOMAS LYNN. 1960. *Fundamental of Population Study.* Philadelphia: J. B. Lippincott.

SPENGLER, JOSEPH J., and OTIS DUDLEY DUNCAN, eds. 1956. *Demographic Analysis, Selected Readings.* New York: The Free Press.

SPIEGELMAN, MORTIMER. 1958. "Mortality trends and prospects and their implications," *Annals of the American Academy,* 316: 25–33.

STAMP, LAURENCE DUDLEY. 1965. *The Geography of Life and Death.* Ithaca, N.Y.: Cornell University Press.

THOMPSON, WARREN S., and D. T. LEWIS. 1965. *Population Problems.* New York: McGraw-Hill.

URBACH, FREDERICK, ed. 1969. *The Biologic Effects of Ultraviolet Radiation, With Emphasis on the Skin.* Elmsford, N.Y.: Pergamon Press.

U. S. Dept. of Commerce, Bureau of Census. 1960. *Historical Statistics of the United States, Colonial Times to 1957.*

U. S. Dept. of Commerce. Monthly vital statistics reports.

WASHBURN, S. L. 1964. "The study of race," in *The Concept of Race,* Ashley Montagu, ed. New York: The Free Press, pp. 242–260.

1969 World Health Statistics Annual, Geneva.

Index

ST. JOHN FISHER COLLEGE LIBRARY
GN62.8 .M64
Molnar, Stephen, 193   010101 000
Races, types, and ethnic group

0 1219 0097458 9

DATE DUE

MAY 0 5 1995	
APR 2 1 2006	
OCT 1 1 2012	

DEMCO, INC. 38-2931